OUT of the DARKNESS

Observations

"When Allison arrived at our facility (National Rehab Hospital, Wash., D.C.), she was in an incredibly fragile physical state, but even so, her indomitable spirit was evident. She persevered through and triumphed over one of the most frightening experiences imaginable--going from a confident independent business woman to being TOTALLY and COMPLETELY reliant on strangers to provide her care: from the mundane to the most intimate aspects of daily life. 'Inspirational' and 'hero' are terms thrown around so frequently and loosely today that their meaning has been diluted. Allison is all of those, but more importantly, she has fought to become 'normal' again."

Lisa M. Maddox, M.D.
The Polytrauma Amputee
Network System Medical Director
Veterans Administration Medical Center

"Allison O'Reilly's story is one of incredible strength and determination. She would not accept lifelong disability, she would not stay 'locked-in'. And all of us who have come to know her are better for it."

Anita Brikman
Former Health Correspondent/Anchor WUSA9

"Stories of miraculous recovery give hope and inspiration to all stroke survivors and their families. This is a story of recovery that is not easily duplicated; a shining example of dedication to recovery and believing in yourself. Anyone touched by the effects of stroke can learn from the bravery and the spirit of Allison."

—Darlene S. Williamson, MA, CCC-SL
Founder and Executive Director, Stroke Comeback Center

"Oh, she's the best outcome I've ever seen after a locked in. That doesn't mean it's good, but it's the best I've ever seen."

—Dr. Nancy Futrell, M.D. Neurology.
Intermountain Stroke Center

Sometimes I think my life would make a great TV movie. It even has the part where they say "Stand by. We are experiencing temporary difficulties."

—Robert Brault

OUT of the DARKNESS

An Inspirational Story of Survival in the
Face of Stroke and Locked-In Syndrome

Allison S. O'Reilly
Stroke Survivor

ARCHWAY
PUBLISHING

Cover Image by: Paul Carson, Carson Creative LLC.

Interior Graphics by: Erik Uecke/Washingtonian Magazine.

Other Interior Images and Author Photo by:
Cal Covert
Owner
Silver Ridge Productions, Inc.

Archway Publishing books may be ordered through booksellers or by contacting:

Archway Publishing
1663 Liberty Drive
Bloomington, IN 47403
www.archwaypublishing.com
1-(888)-242-5904

ISBN: 978-1-4808-0481-4 (sc)
ISBN: 978-1-4808-0483-8 (hc)
ISBN: 978-1-4808-0482-1 (e)

Library of Congress Control Number: 2014902095

Printed in the United States of America

Archway Publishing rev. date: 3/18/2014

For my husband, friends, family, and others whose love, caring thoughts, prayers, and well wishes helped me get through this nightmare and for treating me as normally as possible, while seeing through my disability.

For all Stroke Survivors who have been counted out. May you have the strength and will to be the best you can be.

A friend is someone who understands your past, believes in your future, and accepts you today just the way you are.

—Anonymous

It's not the disability that defines you, it's how you deal with the challenges the disability presents you with.

—Jim Abbott
Former major league pitcher

Table of Contents

Foreword

I was working through my usual day and answered a page about a possible admission to MedStar National Rehabilitation Hospital (MNRH) from a local hospital. It was about an unfortunate younger woman, age forty-nine, who had recently suffered one of the worst types of stroke imaginable—a large brainstem infarction (BSI)—which had given her what's called the *locked-in syndrome*.

A BSI is a stroke that happens when blood cannot flow to your brainstem. The effects of any stroke depend on several factors, including the location of the obstruction and how much brain tissue is affected. However, because each side of the brain controls the opposite side of the body, a stroke affecting one side will result in neurological complications on the side of the body it affects. For example, if the stroke occurs in the brain's right side, the left side of the body (and the left side of the face) will be affected. If the stroke occurs in the left side of the brain, the right side of the body will be affected. When stroke occurs in the *brain stem,* depending on the severity of the injury, it can affect *both sides of the body* and leave someone in a "locked-in" state.

When a locked-in state occurs, the patient is generally unable to speak or achieve any movement below the neck.

Like the author Jean-Dominique Bauby, in his book *The Diving Bell and the Butterfly*,[1] my patient had no ability to move her legs or arms or mouth. She couldn't swallow foods, and she couldn't talk; she had a feeding tube in her stomach and a breathing tube in her neck. She had absolutely no control of her bowel or bladder. She was on a lot of pain and antidepressant medications. She could blink her eyes to give "yes" or "no" responses, but even those blinks needed to be interpreted carefully.

I also was informed that her husband and friends had created and were wearing a red rubber wristband that said "Not Acceptable," implying they would settle for nothing less than the best possible care and the best outcomes, and that an insurance refusal to authorize services or negativistic projections that her future might be bleak would not be tolerated. These bands were created when they were told she should go to a nursing home versus rehab, and this was *not acceptable*. This is the usual recommendation for older stroke patients, but should not be for younger ones.

Even so, I was not enthusiastic about bringing her to MNRH, as I didn't know what we could do for her. This type of stroke can result in a totally dependent human being—like a person with tetraplegia (also known as quadriplegia) from a spinal cord injury in the neck, whose risk of ending up with a very difficult life, in a nursing home, is extremely high. In order to get back home, she would need extraordinary family and psychosocial support. She would require intensive rehabilitation care from an extremely dedicated rehabilitation team who would support her through the agonizingly slow recovery process, if it came. She would need to learn how to control her arms, legs, urinary sphincter and bowel muscles, throat, and mouth all over again. She would have to have health-care insurance that would be willing to pay for months of intensive therapy with only small gains per week, a type of insurance that is very rare these days.

A proposal had been made to the insurance company that we would need a length of stay of at least six weeks. This was accepted, and miraculously, pre-authorization for her admission to MedStar National Rehabilitation Hospital was granted. We made arrangements for her to come.

The patient, who we came to know as Allison, arrived on a Thursday afternoon. She was assigned to a gifted and very dedicated nurse. Very quickly, Allison showed us what an amazing person she was. My enthusiasm for working with her grew rapidly. She showed completely unexpected and unusual motivation to do what she needed to do and fierce determination to avoid crutches like comfort medications and medical attachments/devices. Honestly, Allison changed my whole perspective on working with patients with a nasty stroke like hers. Many stroke and locked-in patients give up when progress slows down or stops. The attitude of the patient is most important.

Almost as soon as she arrived at our facility, she suffered a setback; she needed to be transferred to an acute care hospital, nearby MedStar Washington Hospital Center for evaluation of a possible PNA (pneumonia).

Weakened stroke patients are always more vulnerable to infectious diseases such as pneumonia, which can also come from silent aspiration. Aspiration pneumonia occurs when you inhale food, drink, vomit, or saliva into your lungs. She survived the setback handily and returned to us a week later. Gains far beyond expectations started coming.

Normally, a person breathes air through the nose and mouth and into the lungs. When a person is *intubated*, a tube is placed through the mouth and into the windpipe. A *tracheostomy* is a procedure whereby the surgeon makes a small hole in a patient's neck directly into the windpipe (trachea). Through this hole, a very short tube called a tracheostomy tube is inserted from the surface of the neck directly into the windpipe. The tracheostomy tube is usually about three inches long. A machine is then connected to the tube and *pushes* air through the tube and into the lungs so that the person doesn't have to put any effort into breathing—the machine does all the work of breathing.

A tracheostomy tube can be removed if breathing or the airway improves so that the tube is no longer needed. The easiest way to test whether or not a tracheostomy tube is needed is to put a plug over the opening. If the trachea can be plugged for a long enough time without any problems, it is probably safe to be removed. Allison was told and immediately accepted that she needed to tolerate her throat-breathing–*trachea* tube being plugged for twenty-four hours straight before it could be safely removed from her neck. Once we placed the plug, she was like a badger mother protecting her young: she wouldn't let anyone near the plug to take it out.

When she was strong enough to breathe on her own, the trachea tube was removed, and the hole in her neck completely closed up within a few weeks without need for another surgical procedure. She was successfully *decannulated*—the process whereby a tracheostomy tube is removed once a patient no longer needs it—within a few weeks of arriving back at MNRH. The breathing tube was removed in what I'm pretty sure was a record time. A trachea tube is always temporary, but it was removed quickly considering she was so very sick when arriving. This was the first of many hurdles on her road to recovery.

Allison's swallowing mechanism wasn't working well, and she needed thickened water for safe swallowing. Thickened liquids are often used for people with *dysphagia*, a disorder of swallowing function. The thicker consistency makes it less likely that an individual will aspirate (have it go down the wrong pipe) while they are drinking. Individuals with difficulty swallowing might find liquids cause coughing, spluttering, or even choking, and thickening the drinks enables them to swallow safely. She hated the thickened water and wanted to get back on to regular "thin" water as quickly as possible. She thought intravenous fluids were a torture. We told her she would need to drink sixteen (!) little cups, four ounces each—of thickened liquid a day to get her swallowing mechanism back in shape for thin water and to keep herself properly hydrated in the meantime—in order to avoid intravenous fluids. It became one of Allison's daily holy rituals to drink those sixteen containers for a total of sixty-four ounces—one whole gallon. I've never seen anyone do that before. Thickened liquids don't feel wet; they don't give you a sense of slaking your thirst. Most patients absolutely refuse to even try to drink it, and they end up needing a lot of intravenous fluids. Allison slugged through it and was very rapidly advanced to thin, regular water and all fluids by mouth once she passed the swallow test.

Allison ended up staying with us until March 2011 and made tremendous progress. But at the time of discharge to home, she still required twenty-four-hour physical assistance for all self-care activities and household mobility. She spoke with a *dysarthria* (very slurred speech) and had to be very careful about swallowing her foods and liquids to avoid having things go down the wrong tube and cause choking.

Allison has been as devoted an outpatient worker as she was during her inpatient stay. Over three years later, Allison is now able to walk on her own and even drive. She has resumed participating in the business activities of her husband, is back on the Board of Hospice Cup and helps other stroke survivors. She has written a book, which you hold in your hands.

She continues to work with a personal trainer and undergoes aqua therapy twice a week each and took weekly speech-languagepathology (SLP) sessions to improve her thinking and speaking skills. Every time I see her as an outpatient, she has new accomplishments to show me, much to her and my delight.

Allison is the sort of person that rehabilitation professionals love working with most: she was and is extremely motivated, and her husband and friends are devoted to her and were very appreciative of the work we were doing with her. She patiently, diligently does her exercises on the prescribed schedules. She does all the incredibly hard work that she needs to do to get herself better. She doesn't feel sorry for herself. She believes that she will benefit from her hard work and will eventually return to a fully satisfying life of personal and professional activity. This book is her story ... so far.

—Brendan E. Conroy, MD, FAAPM&R
Medical Director—Stroke Recovery Program
Chief Medical Information Officer
MedStar National Rehabilitation Hospital
Associate Professor of Clinical Rehabilitation Medicine
Georgetown Department of Rehabilitation Medicine

Preface

I am writing *Out of the Darkness* to help other stroke survivors in a similar situation cope with their new realities, provide helpful information for spouses and families, be a non-clinical voice to the medical industry about the needs and desires of younger people experiencing strokes, and provide inspirational insight from someone who has escaped the darkness of locked-in syndrome.

Every stroke is different, and every recovery is different. *Out of the Darkness* is not meant to downplay people's motivation or willingness to recover; it's my story, a first person account of healing from a massive stroke and locked-in syndrome in order to get my life back, as well as, the lessons learned during this devastating time. Certainly, insurance plays a big part, and you must have an advocate, but attitude is also very important.

Like many survivors, I want to use my experience to help other people understand this confusing condition of stroke in younger people. I want something good to come from this.

1

Miracles Do Happen

Life is like a game of cards. The hand that is dealt you is determinism; the way you play it is free will.

—Jawaharal Nehru[2]
Indian politician (1889–1964)

Just when the caterpillar thought the world was over, it became a butterfly ...

—Proverb[3]

PEOPLE SAY I AM A "WALKING MIRACLE." PERHAPS. MY recovery from a stroke was miraculous, and I am very lucky to be alive! But it has taken a lot of hard work, a loving and supportive husband, a core group of dear friends, and a

1

singular goal/determination to push myself in therapy and on my own to work as hard as possible in order to get my life back. Positive attitude, in any recovery, as in life, is extremely important.

I have heard it said that "strokes are like earthquakes— the epicenter of an earthquake and a stroke are very similar in destruction and the rebuild time needed. Using the same metaphor, structural areas are also affected, with disruptions to roadways (blood cells) and telecommunications (nerve cells)."[4]

I doubt if I will ever gain my former life back and be able to return to work again, but I can continue to assist and help my husband Kevin grow his business and do volunteer project work. He changed his career focus for me, which allows him not to travel in order to be with me through my healing process. Before this, he was a consultant in the telecommunications industry, advising wireless operators on their network designs, implementation, and expansion of their networks. The position required an extensive amount of domestic and international travel. About a year after my stroke, he bought into a medical staffing company that matches health-care professionals with various medical facility's needs and left telecommunications. Our market is in metropolitan Washington, DC, which allows him now to be home with me each night. However, I have gained enough independence that Kevin was able to return to his consulting work in the telecommunications industry.

I really miss working! We do not have children, so both our jobs were a very important part of our lives, giving us a sense of pride and accomplishment.

It's still amazing to me how quickly my daily life and identity were taken away. One week, I was a woman engaged in work, family, and the challenges of daily life; then over what should have been a normal weekend, my life radically changed.

In the fall of 2010, my life was full of joy and happiness: blessed with many good friends throughout the country, challenging and fulfilling work, volunteering for worthy causes, and a strong love and friendship with my husband Kevin, whom I had been married to for twenty-two–plus years. You never know how quickly things can change or why. So, be thankful every day and don't take the little things for granted.

It was October 18, 2010. The last thing I remember is the ambulance coming to my house, and then I was unconscious. I don't remember going to the hospital or being transferred to another hospital for surgery. I woke up in the Intensive Care Unit (ICU) with Kevin and my best friend, Lisa, by my side. I opened my eyes, but could not move any part of my body; I was terrified and had no idea what was ahead.

My ICU nurse, Val, was wonderful! She looked down at me and then looked at them and said, "You know, I think she might still be there. Let's see; talk to her." Val guided conversations in the form of questions, explaining I should blink once for "yes" and twice for "no" answers.

Later, Kevin explained to me that I had had a stroke, undergone surgery and was in the ICU at INOVA Fairfax hospital. Other people began to arrive as well, including my cousin who hates hospitals. His being there made me think I was dying. This also happened when a rabbi was just walking the hospital floor and stopped in to cheer me up! I didn't like men visiting and seeing me in this condition, probably a vanity thing. This became very clear to Kevin, Lisa, and Val as they began to see how I became agitated when a lot of people were around. It was all very confusing as I lay there trying to figure out how I ended up in this situation.

2

Life before the Darkness

It does not matter how slowly you go, so long
as you do not stop.

—Confucius

I WAS BORN IN HONOLULU IN THE SAME HOSPITAL AS
President Obama. My dad worked for a bank. We were only
there until I was two, so I really don't remember that much.
My mom always said I loved the beach and sun because she
would go to the ocean while pregnant. She also took me there
often when I was a baby. We then moved back to Maryland
where she grew up, near my grandparents, as my parents were
getting divorced.

Although my dad was a successful lawyer, he failed to pay
child support, and this did not sit well with my family. My

mother returned to work then, and I was raised largely by my grandparents. My mom has two younger siblings, a brother and a sister. I was the oldest grandchild and the only girl—all my cousins are boys—plus, they raised me and therefore, I became a favorite of my grandparents.

My childhood was full of life. In addition to school, I took ballet and jazz and art classes at the Corcoran Gallery of Art on the Washington Mall. Being near DC was wonderful. I had bowling and Putt-Putt birthday parties. Some Saturdays, I was also fortunate to go horseback riding with my father in Rock Creek Park and rode a horse named Crackerbarrel. I recall my Sweet Sixteen party with friends and family, where my uncle gave me a beautiful strand of pearls and my mom gave me a platinum, diamond, and emerald ring that was passed down from my grandmother. My grandfather gave it to my grandmother when their families met for the first time.

My grandfather was an immigrant from Russia who earned a law degree and went on to own and manage several liquor stores in and around Washington, DC. His work hours were long, and he did not get home most nights until 10:30 p.m. My grandmother would feed him a big meal, and then he would go to bed on a full stomach. When relaxing, he smoked a cigar and a pipe. My grandmother had a sweet tooth and loved Hershey's kisses. She would always leave a trail of the silver wrappings to their bedroom.

My grandmother would have planned meals on certain days. For example, Monday's were lamb chops, homemade French fries, and carrots. My friends would love to come over after school; we made ice cream sundaes and watched *General Hospital,* my grandmother's favorite soap opera. I got my first car, a 1972 yellow Firebird at age sixteen and a half. My mom bought it for $2,500, but I was responsible for gas, insurance, maintenance, etc. It had air conditioning, leatherette seats, and an eight-track player. It was my pride and joy. I had the same boyfriend throughout high school who took me to homecoming and prom. To earn money, I worked as a lifeguard in the summer at our apartment pool and on Saturdays at my uncle's optometry office.

I graduated high school a year early, missing my senior year. All I needed was English, so I took it in the summer. My birthday is in September, so I was just shy of seventeen when I graduated high school. I then went to Montgomery College for two years and then the University of Maryland.

My mom had gotten remarried when I was fifteen at my aunt's house in Silver Spring, MD. I then went to live with my mom and stepdad, Lou, after graduation from high school. I was happy for my mom as she would now have someone to grow old with and make special memories. Lou was in the printing business and was five years younger than my mom. He was about five-foot-nine, nice looking, and wore glasses. He had a sweet smile and a hearty laugh. Lou was wonderful to me and wanted to adopt me. Being fifteen and knowing one day I would get married, and change my name again, I declined. Besides, I didn't need to be adopted to know who my *dad* was. We had wonderful family barbeques, decorated the house and a tree for Christmas, and enjoyed many special occasions as a family. I also looked forward to our tree decorating party we had each Christmas."

My favorite aunt lived in South Florida, so I would visit her during school breaks and moved there after school.

7

I worked during the week and went to the beach every weekend. I worked at the World of Palm Aire in Pompano Beach, which was a big, popular spa at that time. It is now a Wyndham hotel. Sometimes my aunt and I would fly to the Bahamas for the evening and go gambling, as the gambling age there was eighteen. She loved the slots; I loved blackjack. I still do! What an exciting time in my life.

While living in Florida, I met a guy who lived next door to my aunt. Joe and I dated and after some time, we moved in together. Shortly thereafter, he asked me to marry him. I said no! Although I loved him, his extended family was in the mob in New York. We continued to struggle for money and he for a steady job. That was not what I wanted. He was involved in many shady things, which was completely out of character for me. We loved each other so much, but in my heart, I knew better and decided to move back to DC. After I moved home, Joe became involved in some criminal activities and was in jail in Haiti. After returning from Florida, I lived at home and then moved into a townhouse with two girlfriends. I met them through a good friend, who was a sorority sister of theirs at Ohio State University; coincidentally, that's where my husband went to college. While living with them in Maryland, I came home from a bridal shower, and my roommates told me two men in suits from the Drug Enforcement Agency (DEA) had stopped by looking to speak with me. I was scared. A few minutes later, the doorbell rang—the DEA agents had waited for me to get home. The DEA thought I was his Washington, DC, connection. Joe had called me to ask for help and just to hear my voice. I would call the jail to speak with him.

I couldn't imagine the loneliness, being so scared, and the jail being in such a terrible condition. At the time I worked at the long-distance telephone company MCI (Microwave Communications Incorporated) and my boss's wife was a lawyer and an angel in this scary situation. She represented me at the grand jury hearing. I was finally cleared, and my life went on.

Speaking of my boss, I had always worked—for as long as I can remember—and had always been an enthusiastic employee throughout my career. For twenty-five plus years I worked in marketing and advertising, mostly in telecommunications and hospitality organizations. But my first job, when I was twenty-one, was at MCI, the first real competition for AT&T. It was just the beginning of the soon-to-explode telecommunications boom, and MCI was instrumental in the legal and regulatory changes that led to the breakup of AT&T as the telephone monopoly and ushered in the competitive long-distance telephone industry. It became MCI WorldCom in 1998 and two years later just WorldCom. My positions were in advertising, marketing, and promotions. I started my career as a coordinator and ended it as a director of marketing and communications. I was at MCI for eight years—until I moved to Boston. I am still friends with my boss and coworkers from those days; telecom is a small world.

Through my career, I had excellent performance reviews and was promoted with increased responsibilities, larger teams, and bigger assignments to manage. While working at Nextel, I won the Circle of Excellence Award (their highest achievement), being the only one in marketing to do so that year. I was fortunate to have worked with a number of wonderful people, many who have become great friends and have reached out to me frequently throughout my recovery.

———◇———

I met my husband, Kevin, over thirty years ago, when I was just twenty-one. He was twenty-nine and looked so handsome in the tuxedo he was wearing to help a friend of his host a business party at his jewelry store. I knew immediately we were meant for each other—it was love at first sight for both of us. We talked when he was not working the party and went out after the party ended. He then asked me out on a real date. I knew ... he was *the one.* I had butterflies and all the tell-tale signs of being in love.

But he also broke my heart during our dating years, as I wanted to get married but he did not. He was married for almost three years prior and was getting divorced when we met and was not looking to enter into another relationship. We dated off and on for eight years before finally getting engaged. Kevin has a distinctive voice, and when he would call me at work, people would say, "The man with the nice voice called." I loved his presence and positive influence on my life.

While living with my roommates, we would all watch Ohio State football on Saturdays and attended a few games in Columbus as well. As you will see, the Buckeyes became an important part of our lives. Kevin said I should live alone before getting married, which was great advice. He wanted me to know what it was like to be totally responsible for a household. I moved into a one-bedroom apartment. It was adorable. I loved it, and it was all mine! It was decorated beautifully, and I was responsible for everything. My mom, however, was not happy I had my own apartment. Although she was proud to see me paying for it all by myself, having my own apartment meant I was not going to move home again. My mom didn't want things to change that much—she still saw me as her little girl.

It took seven years for Kevin and I to move in together, almost a year after to be engaged, and nine months to get married. We do not have children—neither of us ever had a driving desire for them, which I think you need to be a good parent. Kevin's parents were much older, and I am an only child, so being around children was not familiar. People who have kids think this is strange, but believe me, millions of perfectly happy and healthy adults choose not to be parents. We have made our own family from our friends.

Although it took him awhile to say, "I do," I could always feel his true love and commitment. This year, we have known each other thirty-one years, and we still tell each other "I love you" every day. This goes beyond wedding vows—in sickness and in health. Because no one can imagine what that means until sickness occurs for real. A stroke can happen to anyone, and it takes enormous love and commitment for the partner to get through it, never mind the stroke survivor. In the best of circumstances, marriage is challenging. When one partner has a stroke, both partners have a stroke. My job now is to continue progressing my independence and not be a burden on my husband, family, or friends.

When I was in the hospital, I would think and tell Kevin, "I'm a bad wife." This kind of thought is common to someone seriously ill, as you are not the same as you were, as much as you try. One thing that differentiates a stroke from other devastating illnesses is that it is so abrupt and that it sometimes occurs relatively early in life. I used to run all the errands, grocery shop, clean the house, etc., and now Kevin and I both do it. I liked being responsible for my household chores. While a stroke can create strain, frustration, and distance in your marriage, coping with its effects is an opportunity to reset your priorities and goals. You may be able to strengthen your marriage as you work together on common problems you will face. It is by accepting the limitations that life imposes on us that we can overcome them.

Allison and Kevin walk
May 2012

In 1986, Kevin took a new job and moved from Washington, DC, to Philadelphia. We commuted on the weekends to see each other, alternating the drive. A few years later, he was offered a wonderful position up in Boston, and in 1988, Kevin moved again. He wanted to live by the water, so he settled in the town of Marblehead on the Massachusetts North Shore, which also had easy access to the airport, which he needed for the job. A forty-minute drive north of Boston and just east of infamous Salem, Massachusetts, Marblehead is a jewel. Called the "yachting capital of America," it is the birthplace of the United States Navy. I thought to myself, *This is perfect; he'll never meet anyone in this sleepy little town.*

The day Kevin and I traveled up to Marblehead to look for an apartment for him, there was a classic *nor'easter* snowstorm coming up the east coast. Flights were canceled, so we took Amtrak. We got the last rental car and followed a snow plow to Marblehead. When we got to the Harbor Light Inn, the owner said, "Just plow the car in the driveway." Since no one could drive, we walked everywhere around town during the weekend.

A year later, we met in New York City for a romantic weekend, and he asked me to move to Boston. No ring, though, or promise of marriage. But still, I gave up friends, family, and a secure job. I had no choice—I had to try! We decided I would move up in six months. That would give my parents time to get used to the idea and for me to stay in my job at MCI a little longer. I had been there almost eight years.

It was Halloween 1989 when I moved to Boston. I had a job upon my arrival. The prospective company called my boss Judy, for a reference, she told me, "I gave you a great reference, but you won't like the job." She was right. She recommended I meet with a friend who could help with a job search. He told me to write blindly and send my resume cold—which would not work today—to companies in the Boston area that I found interesting.

One company I heard from was ITT Sheraton. I loved the hiring manager and got a good vibe. He told me the job was between me and a man who had hospitality experience. I did not! I had a follow-up interview on a Wednesday. I had resigned from my current job the previous Friday—resigning before I got the offer. Kevin thought I was crazy. I went on the interview, was hired, and started the next day. When asked if I had hospitality experience, I said, "Well, I have stayed in hotels!" My work experience and can-do attitude played a big part in me being hired.

The hospitality business was very enjoyable. A few years after working in marketing for Sheraton, I was hired by an advertising agency that specialized in the hospitality industry. My account was the Four Seasons Hotels and Resorts, headquartered in Toronto, Ontario. These clients were terrific. I liked having the agency experience, and it proved helpful in my work experience down the road. Having worked at both the client and agency end was invaluable.

In addition to corporate marketing, I had responsibility to promote individual hotels in the United States too. I opened the Four Seasons Hotel New York, and after each hurricane season and subsequent rebuild, I promoted the Four Seasons Resort, Nevis, in the West Indies. I was responsible for driving business using print ads, brochures, and direct mail. Increasing business in hotel restaurants and bars, meetings and events, and finding partners that were similar to the Four Seasons customer also fell to me. Hospitality advertising and marketing was very different from telecommunications, much more about fun and romance than efficiency and price points. I loved it.

In 1991, Kevin and I were married in Washington, DC, a year and a half after my move to Boston. Our maid of honor, best man, and the groom all went to Ohio State. So, I was made an Honorary Buckeye! We had a beautiful wedding at what is now the St. Regis in DC. We had a rabbi and a minister, both from the Georgetown University Theology department. We met with the rabbi prior to our wedding at his home in Martha's Vineyard. At the time, there were not many interfaith couples.

I don't think Kevin's family had ever been to a Jewish wedding or knew anyone who was Jewish. We married under a *chuppah*, or bridal canopy; we broke the glass; my grandfather blessed the challah bread, and we danced the traditional Jewish dance, the *hora*, or chair dance. Kevin was overwhelmed and amused when his friends lifted him up. We signed the *ketubah* or marriage contract, witnessed by the best man and maid of honor, and lit the unity candle. My mom and grandparents, Kevin's mom, and others were there. It's nice to look back at the DVD and remember.

We were married in October but did not take our honeymoon until February. We went to Rio de Janeiro for *Carnaval*—not your traditional honeymoon destination. I was a bit naïve in what to expect, as I had not traveled out of the country, except to the Caribbean. But Kevin and a friend had gone to the Amazon rainforest and Rio a year earlier and loved it. Our hotel was on Copacabana Beach and near Ipanema Beach. We met great people, who are still our friends. We went sightseeing, went to Carnaval parties, and did all the things tourists do. The beaches, people, and food were wonderful.

Back at home in Marblehead, we lived in this beautiful New England town on the ocean for nine years and really loved it. I commuted each day to Newbury Street in Boston, which was over an hour away, but to see the ocean each and every day was a gift. We knew no one when we first moved there, so it was wonderful to build a life together—just us. We made special friends, bought our first house, and had amazing neighbors, who we still visit with every July Fourth holiday. I had a beach pass to Devereaux beach. It's a rocky beach, but a beach, nonetheless. Heaven! We joined the Corinthian Yacht Club, sailed, and sat on their big wraparound porch in rocking chairs, drinking cocktails overlooking the thriving harbor. Life was exciting; we had "made it," and we were young and in good health.

My mom and Lou joined us in the Boston area in 1994, as Lou's printing job was coincidentally transferred north. My mom was thrilled and thought we would do things together all the time now that we were near each other. They lived in North Andover, which is only about a half hour from Marblehead. But I worked more than full time, and Kevin and I had built a new life together that was also quite full. The weather was also not welcoming. In 1996, we moved my parents back to Maryland, again for Lou's job and, probably, my mom's sanity.

I met a good friend, a neighbor, Darryll, and we would go to the beach together on the weekends. Kevin would *visit* us, riding his bike or running around Marblehead Neck. Darryll would make us gourmet lunches. Darryll and I would go on vacation together to South Beach, Florida. We were the original *Will & Grace*, but I was married. We had so much fun together. I called Darryll my "beach husband."

Being near Salem, famous for its seventeenth-century witch trials, was fun too, especially at Halloween. Once we celebrated Halloween at a Halloween Ball and won a prize for going as Billiard Balls—eight colored balls, the eight ball, and a cue stick. It was a memorable time.

The summers and falls in New England are gorgeous; the winters, unfortunately, are too cold and too long. Eventually, we moved back to the DC area, moving to McLean, Virginia.

———◁◦▷———

Kevin and I were fortunate enough to travel domestically and throughout the world. Every five years, we drove from La Jolla, California to San Francisco, along coastal Highway 1. We would go to the Hamptons in New York for the weekend and down to Naples, Florida, frequently.

We traveled to London in May 1997. Since the Four Seasons Hotel London was my account, we stayed there when visiting. The director of marketing asked us to stay an extra day to meet Princess Diana, who was coming to the hotel for tea, but we had to go home and could not stay. She died in August, a tragedy and a missed opportunity for us.

Kevin and I worked hard, saved our money, and eventually had two beautiful homes—our main house in McLean, Virginia, and a vacation home in Naples, Florida, on Florida's Gulf Coast. We were very fortunate and knew we were "living the charmed life."

We had planned to go to Italy (Venice, Florence, Rome, and the Amalfi Coast) for our tenth anniversary, but that was just after 9/11 tragedy, and no one was traveling. We drove to

Charleston, South Carolina, and Savannah, Georgia, instead. They were charming. We eventually made it to Italy in 2005. In spring 2010 we went to France (Paris, Lyon, Provence, Nice, Monte Carlo, Cannes, and St. Tropez) to celebrate our twentieth anniversary early. We walked and walked and walked … maybe five to eight miles a day. I had to buy *chippies*, which are like sneakers so that I could prevent bad blisters and still wear my heels in the evening. I played blackjack at the famous Monte Carlo Casino. The man next to me wore a tuxedo—very James Bond. I won enough for our cab fare back to Nice. Although it was a year before our actual anniversary, we had decided to go because we had the time and always liked to live our lives in the moment. Thank goodness we did, because only a few months later, everything would be changed.

We would go to Martha's Vineyard each year, whether we lived in Massachusetts or Virginia. We would go Labor Day weekend, and more often than not, a storm would hit Labor Day, ending the New England island summer in a gust. We met people at the Edgartown Inn each year, and we would catch up on life. We met up with friends for dinner, even staying at their homes and getting the *real Vineyard experience*. You had to walk through a marsh to get to the private beach. We would be the only ones there. It was glorious. They also had an outdoor shower at the beach, which was an experience for a city girl.

————◆————

Wherever we lived, we had wonderful parties that went on into the wee hours, and the O'Reilly's became known for our traditional Christmas Party. People living in Boston even came in a snowstorm. We decorated the house extensively for the holidays. Kevin thought I went a bit too far. But, what would you expect from a nice Jewish girl. I love Christmas! Maybe it's just the widespread festive atmosphere or being an only child—from when I was little, even birthdays were always important, and celebrating a big deal.

Kevin had planned a surprise party for my fortieth birthday, but, like our anniversary trip, it too was canceled by the 9/11 tragedy. Our friends from Marblehead, John and Cheri, flew down anyway, and we went to dinner with them, along with our DC friends, Lisa and Greg. It was perfect, exactly what I wanted for my birthday, considering the shock we were all in.

Cheri had sent a huge box to the house a few weeks prior to my birthday. She said not to open it until she was there. It was forty shoes—twenty pair, each individually wrapped. All kinds of shoes: slippers, sandals, heels, boots, tennis shoes. What a great gift. When I would wear them, I called them "Cheri Shoes."

September 2011 was my fiftieth birthday. Although I was released from the MNRH in March and still in recovery, I planned a five-day all-inclusive trip to Sandals in Exuma Bay, the Bahamas. We had four other couples joining us; it was perfect. Because my fortieth birthday had been canceled, and now the stroke was behind me, this celebration was extra special. We had a wonderful celebration dinner with a dedicated staff, who delivered a yummy coconut birthday cake (my favorite) and sang to me. Lisa had the room decorated with balloons and flowers. The resort had a swim-up bar, and we played 1980s Trivia. Our group was very competitive! There was breathtaking golf for many attendees, though not me, and Lisa took me to the beach and pool where we had piña coladas. We were in a handicap room, and we had a butler who brought us around the resort on a golf cart, as it was difficult for me to get around. At that time, I had a walker. I could not have imagined this as just months before I was still in the hospital.

In February 2003, I had planned Kevin's fiftieth birthday party in Las Vegas at my favorite hotel, the Bellagio. He was completely surprised by twenty-six people coming from all over the country.

In February 2013, I had a surprise party for his sixtieth birthday. I did it again: he had no clue! We had dinner for thirty people at the Palm Restaurant in McLean, Virginia. Again, people came from all over, including his friend from Spain. Everyone said he would be mad at me, but I wanted him to have a special day and thank him for being so wonderful, especially over the last two-plus years.

In the summer of 1997, Kevin got a call about a job in DC and the position would report to a woman I had worked with at MCI. Small world. I saw this as a positive sign.

The move was easy, the job great, and we found a beautiful house in McLean, Virginia, just outside the capital. Being raised in Maryland, this was a big move. People in Maryland don't go to Virginia and people in Virginia don't go to Maryland, even though it's just across the river. And neither go to DC, except for work or when you have company visiting from out of town. Weird.

Kevin had asked if we could live in Virginia, and I'd said

yes, although I didn't know anything about it. Virginia was foreign to me. I got a job at Nextel Communications, which was based in McLean and less than two miles away from our house. Nextel was a wireless provider that later merged and became a subsidiary of the Sprint Corporation. It was still just the beginning of wireless. I remember calling Kevin and telling him I had found my people. I was back in telecom, and there were other former MCI'ers there too. I worked there for eight years—until just after the merger with Sprint. I made forever friends and had wonderful managers and leadership. I left Sprint Nextel in December 2005 ... because of the merger.

I worked at a few places after the merger and was consulting for over a year before the stroke.

I met my best friend Lisa on my first day at Nextel, and I knew we'd be friends forever. People would always ask if we were sisters. Tired of the question, we started saying yes. We *felt* like sisters. I would do anything for her and she for me. She hardly left my or Kevin's side during the early days of the stroke.

For her fiftieth birthday, Kevin and I, and two other couples, joined Lisa and her husband on a rented houseboat on Lake Powell for five days. What fun! Not far from Vegas, Lake Powell is a reservoir on the Colorado River, straddling the border between Utah and Arizona. Though it was her birthday, everyone was very loving and accommodating to my needs. We went in the lake—Lisa having bought me my own life vest. Kevin was adamant about me not going down the slide off the top deck; rather, I should use the steps in the back of the boat. We visited the Rainbow Bridge, on the

Utah side. I could not walk the entire way, but with Kevin's help, far enough to see it. The bridge is really beautiful. On the way home, we went to Las Vegas for a few days. It was a great change of scenery and showed that even after the stroke, you must keep living.

A similar houseboat on Lake Powell
September 2012

In 2008, we downsized from a single family home to a townhome about a mile from our original house in McLean. It is four stories—built-in therapy. We were very involved in its construction and got to customize it for our needs. Before being discharged from MNRH, I needed to provide my physical therapist, Stacey, with pictures of the house to ensure it was safe. Kevin thought we needed to install a chair lift, but Stacey said no. Additional handrails on the stairs, toilet-seat railings, and a shower seat were all that I needed.

I have never liked elevators, so I had walked up the steps to my office and anywhere else where I had the choice. It kept me in shape and was an unexpected benefit in my rehabilitation.

Kevin often calls me a rules person, because I do what's right and don't challenge the rules. I go to the doctor each year; I don't smoke; I don't have high blood pressure or high cholesterol; I am not overweight, and I don't drink a lot. Birth control pills were my only … vice.

Being an only child, I'd grown up with some life-imposing pressures on me. My mom was chronically sick, almost always heavy, and eventually developed diverticulitis. In October 2010, she had a colostomy and was in the hospital longer than she should have been due to complications, her weight did not help. The doctor who did the surgery said, "Your mother is obese." It was the first time I'd heard anyone say what I guess I'd known but hadn't wanted to believe. Until you decide you want to lose weight, nothing will happen.

My stepdad, Lou, also had health problems. He'd had some symptoms similar to Alzheimer's—forgetfulness, a shuffle when walking, to name two. A visit to the ER determined it was *hydrocephalus,* fluid on the brain. He had a shunt put in to drain the fluid off, but he lost his ability to drive. My mom was now the caregiver. When she got sick, I managed paying their monthly bills (including giving them a large amount of money each month), cleaning their house, taking Lou to the grocery store, and more—all while working over forty hours a week. I was trying my best to balance everything that was put on me … but it proved to be too much for me. It was never enough for my mom, and she often told me so. I paid no attention to her, as I knew there was only so much of me to go around.

Because of being an only child, I dealt with a lot of stress—there was no one to turn to; everything always fell on my shoulders. I got to dreading the phone ringing, and even seeing my mom sometimes ended in both of us being upset.

There were good times too. My mom had good friends and visited with them often. She had a big personality and a great laugh. She often felt entitled, though, and this bothered me and many others as well. It had a lot to do with how she was raised—spoiled. As the oldest, she was basically raised as an only child for four years, and then as the only girl for ten years. Whatever the reason, while my mom was growing up, "no" was rarely said to her.

My mom carried all her weight in her middle and had very thin legs. She had fallen and broken her femur (the thigh bone), and had a hip replacement because of her weight. Both of her surgeries and Lou's surgery required stays at a rehabilitation facility. This was before my stroke, and I had done my research, finding a great rehab location.

A year later, 2009, Lou needed another shunt, as the symptoms came back. And again he went to the same facility.

I knew my mom and Lou could no longer live on their own in their condo. So, Kevin and I began searching independent-living options in the area. I came close to narrowing them down, but the cost was high.

Kevin and my mom never did really get along. The only

thing they had in common was me, whom they both loved. I think, having only one child, my mom didn't want to share me, and wanted me to choose who I loved more and give my time to her instead. I loved them differently, of course, and it was not fair to make me choose. But I did! I grew to be more independent and to live my life as I wanted. Kevin was my one true love.

Because Kevin broke my heart a lot in the beginning of our relationship, my mom did not feel he was right for me. She wanted me to marry a doctor and have children, lunch during the week with girlfriends maybe, but, most important, see more of her. She did not want me to work, and working forty-plus hours a week did not leave a lot of time for visiting her—which she told me frequently.

After the colostomy surgery, she was very unhappy in the hospital and wanted to escape. At times, she had to be restrained. She was a terrible patient. You are not allowed to leave the hospital until you are released. I put everything in order for her to go into rehab once she was released. That was to be Monday, October 18, 2010.

Meanwhile, Kevin has one sister, eleven month's younger than he. Because they are Irish Catholic, they tell everyone they're Irish twins, being only eleven months apart! His dad died of throat cancer when he was fourteen, and his mom passed away about nine years after we got married.

Friends are the family you are fortunate to pick yourself! Kevin's friends are very important to him and he speaks to them on a regular basis—I always tell him he's like a woman this way!

———◄◦►———

I have recently had childhood girlfriends reach out and re-engage in my life. A friend from middle school, Suzanne, ran into another friend, Jenny, while shopping. When told about what had happened, she was stunned. She called and e-mailed me immediately. Another middle-school friend of ours is back in my life too. Today, Suzanne takes me twice a week to my pool therapy, doctor appointments, the nail and hair salon, and to do errands. It's hard being dependent on people, and I so appreciate her. We have been friends a long time, and it seems like no time has passed. Everything is easy because it's familiar … we picked up right away. I am happy and thankful to have them back in my life. It brings some sense of normalcy to see them. It is said good friends are people you know and don't need to talk to every single day. You don't even need to talk to each other for weeks—and in our case, years—but when you do, it's like you never stopped talking.

A few years ago, Kevin had skin cancer on his nose. It was a basal cancer (the best of the worst cancer). After the lesion was removed, he needed plastic surgery. When the doctor's office told me the things that could happen with anesthesia, including death, I started crying. I couldn't imagine my life without Kevin—he was my rock. At the time, I was his Florence Nightingale, and now he is mine. He has recovered and is careful in the sun.

In the fall of 2010, I had just had my yearly physical and was given a clean bill of health. I had a very charmed life at the age of forty-nine. That life was about to change in an instant!

3

The Stroke and Next Steps

I WAS WORKING SIXTY-PLUS HOURS A WEEK, VISITING MY mom in the hospital each night, talking with her doctors throughout each day, paying Lou's bills, taking Lou to visit my mom, to go to the grocery store, and to run errands. Their neighbors were helpful, but they had their lives to live.

As I said, my mom was a terrible patient and had to be restrained at times. She would call the nurses' names, make rude comments, and did not like waiting to be tended to. She would pull out her IVs, and she was allergic to many medicines, making feeling better difficult. I was exhausted and dreaded visiting. My aunt and uncle used to joke that I was a saint and had paid my dues over and over. That's where being an only child comes into play. Who else is going to do it?

On Saturday night, October 16, 2010, for a change of scenery, I spent the night at my girlfriend Lisa's house while Kevin was away in Arizona playing golf with Lisa's husband. We had a family-style dinner with her three girls, a couple of cocktails, and watched *Scooby Doo*. It was a great, relaxing evening!

The next morning, I had breakfast and set out for home. There was nothing out of the ordinary. When I got home, my mom had left a message that she was ready to escape from the hospital. I called her back, as she had forgotten I had spent the night at Lisa's. She yelled at me, telling me I was a terrible daughter. I knew she did not mean this; she was just so tired of the hospital. She told me to come by, and I did so, to try to calm her down.

After the hospital visit, I went to do some household things for Lou, and I suddenly had a terrible pain up and down my left arm. He tried to get me to stay, but I really wanted to get home. I arrived home, and the pain stopped. I cleaned the house, which to me was like therapy. Later that evening, I spoke to our friend and dentist, Brian, and said I didn't feel well. He thought it was because I had not eaten. Then later, the room started to spin. I also had a terrible ringing in my ear and nausea. I just didn't feel right. I called my neighbors (Gisela and her husband, Richard) and asked them to come over, as Kevin was on a flight from Arizona. I unlocked the door for my neighbors to come in, holding on to furniture to maintain balance as the room was spinning, and went back onto the bathroom floor. Upon entering the house and seeing me on the bathroom floor, they said either they were taking me to the emergency room or calling 911. They immediately helped me down the front stairs and we were on our way; the hospital was ten to fifteen minutes away. Gisela thought I was having a heart attack. It was late, and the ER was somewhat full. She told the attending nurse, "You must take care of my friend now!" They did a test and ruled out a heart attack.

Next, they did a CT scan (which I don't remember) and said I had vertigo and was dehydrated. They gave me fluids. Kevin arrived around midnight, and around 2:30 a.m., they released me from the hospital and sent me home with prescriptions to be filled in the morning. The ER did not do the standard test to confirm vertigo or rule out a stroke. I was wheeled out and helped into the passenger side of the Kevin's car, so I never walked. Kevin helped me up the stairs, almost carrying me. He helped me change into my nightgown, and as I am a workaholic, he said, "No argument, you're not going to work for at least two days." Ha! Again, he almost had to carry me to the restroom about 4:30 a.m., as I was weak and had very little, if any, balance. Feeling very weak is what the hospital had said to expect.

Before going to fill the prescriptions in the morning, Kevin tried to give me some juice, so I would be hydrated. It just ran down my chin as I could not swallow. My eyes were wide open, and my hands and feet clenched into a ball—a classic sign of a stroke.

Kevin called 911 and then Gisela to see if I was in the same condition as the night before. She answered, "She is much worse." All I remember is the ambulance coming and four handsome guys from the McLean Volunteer Fire Department taking me out of the house, down the front steps on a stretcher, and saying they thought I was having a stroke.

Six hours after being discharged, I was wheeled on a stretcher into the same hospital, unconscious, and after an MRI, diagnosed with a brain stem stroke.

Kevin followed the ambulance in his car. It was the beginning of my feeling so alone and scared. Kevin called my best friend, Lisa, who met him at the hospital. The MRI showed a clot in the brain stem, but because of the rarity of where the clot was, that hospital could not do the surgery. They sent me to another hospital that could do the surgery immediately. It was about sixteen hours after onset before I had surgery, which is a long time.

As explained by the National Stroke Association, recognizing symptoms and acting *fast* to get medical attention can save a life and limit disabilities. If given within three hours of the first symptom, there is an FDA-approved clot-buster medication that might reduce long-term disability for the most common type of stroke. As with other strokes, early treatment is essential, with the prognosis being the best if the patient can be treated within hours of the suspected stroke.

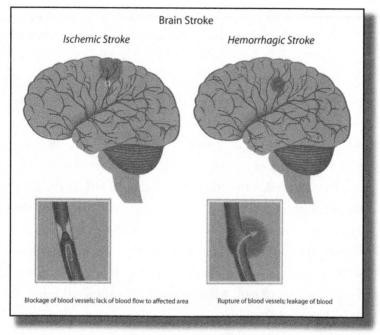

The two types of strokes (Shutterstock.com)

In a recent John Hopkins study, "Diagnosing the vast majority of strokes—ischemic strokes, which occur when blood flow is cut off from part of the brain—a CT is the wrong diagnostic tool, missing an estimated 85 percent of strokes in the first twenty-four hours after symptoms begin, and about 60 percent in the days that follow." About one in three strokes whose primary symptom is dizziness is missed in the emergency room, sometimes with tragic consequences, including preventable deaths."[5]

Shortly after confirming my trip to the ER was not about vertigo, but something much more serious, Kevin had to notify everyone, get Power of Attorney, obtain my passwords, and more. He also learned all the things I had been doing for my mom and Lou, which included daily visits to the hospital to see her, daily talks with her doctors, and coordination with the rehab facility once she would be released.

You never know how people will react to a life-altering event. Kevin and Lisa were scared when told I needed life-saving surgery. The doctor gave three possible outcomes—two would have resulted in my death and one was the successful removal of the clot, which occurred. Thank goodness!

That same day my mom was being moved to the rehab facility. Kevin told her and Lou that I was exhausted and that was why I wasn't there. A day later, he told them it was more serious and that I was in the hospital but would not say where, so they could not find out how serious my condition was. They were devastated. My mom started calling all hospitals in and around Washington, DC, looking for me. Kevin was mentally and physically exhausted running between my mom in rehab and me in the hospital.

Locked-In Syndrome[6]

Imagine lying there, unmoving, totally paralyzed—and your only way of telling people "I'm not dead. I'm still here!" is the blink of your eyes. It's like being buried alive—but with help, you have breathing capabilities. I understood everything, but could not communicate. I was what doctors refer to as "locked-in." Being locked-in was immediate; it was part of the stroke. I could only blink my eyes, so communication was formed as questions, with yes or no answers by blinking: one blink for yes, two blinks for no. I was scared and did not know when the nightmare would end.

Locked-in syndrome (LIS) refers to a very rare outcome (only a few hundred cases are known worldwide) of stroke, caused by a stroke in a small but important area of the brain. This area, located in the brain stem, is a conduit zone for the brain's motor pathways. It is different from other strokes in both its location and severity. The brain stem maintains breathing, houses the cranial nerves, and contains nerve pathways that connect your upper brain to the spinal cord. Individuals with LIS are conscious and can think and reason, but are unable to speak or move. The disorder leaves individuals completely mute and paralyzed.

Persons with LIS can communicate using a communications board via an alphabetical code. My speech therapist at MNRH, Lauren, introduced me to a communications board to use. A person goes up, down, and across the columns with the alphabet, and the patient blinks at the right letter. The letters form a word or words as a way to communicate—not the easiest, and patience is required. Lauren also created a book of visuals of commonly used items to point to as well. This was not used for long, as I made rapid progress.

"You can *feel* all sensations. You can *feel* every touch on your body but are unable to move; all you can do is blink or roll your eyes up and down."

Luckily, brain plasticity, also known as neuroplasticity, suggests that the location of a given function in the brain (for example, speech) can move to another area of the brain. This transfer can be activated by repetitive learning. In the case of stroke, brain plasticity refers to healthy brain cells taking over the functions of damaged brain cells.

LIS is often mistaken as being the same as being in a vegetative state, which is when people can open their eyes but are not aware of their environment. In locked-in syndrome, the person is fully aware of her environment, but cannot talk or move. In truth, you look different, have an empty look, and can't do anything, but you are still the same person inside.

LIS is the most severe neurological condition to be admitted into hospital settings. Individuals with LIS have the highest level of disability among stroke survivors. Early recognition of the LIS state is important for rehabilitation. It is essential that these patients play an active role in decision-making processes regarding their rehabilitation (through blinking). LIS affects around 1 percent of stroke patients.

For those who have had a stroke, there is no cure for locked-in syndrome, nor is there a standard course of treatment. It is extremely rare for patients to recover any significant motor functions. About 90 percent die within four months of its onset.

In a classic, complete locked-in syndrome, the ability to move all the limbs, the trunk, the neck and even muscles of the face is completely destroyed; you lie completely motionless and devoid of expression and speech. Breathing may or may not be impaired. Some people may need the assistance of a breathing tube and a respirator machine. Feeding must be given by a tube in the stomach. I had both.

Though, surprisingly, never in pain, it took awhile to get used to the idea of being fed through a feeding tube. You begin to realize how much you have to depend on other people—to get dressed, wash, scratch an itch, everything.

Being completely dependent on other people is a terrible adjustment to make. It takes time, even though everybody is so willing to help.

Some LIS cases will recover some of their motor skills over time. However, spasticity is a major issue for many stroke survivors. Spasticity is like a "wicked charley horse."[7] Brain injury from stroke sometimes causes muscles to involuntarily contract (shorten or flex) when you try to move your limb. This creates stiffness and tightness. I am very lucky as I do not have this, although my right leg does not like to bend—my hamstring is weak. If I were sitting down, you would never even know I had had a stroke.

But at the time, I'd lay awake in bed, unable to move anything. I had no pressure even in my fingertips. I was hooked up to drips and machines. Nurses would come and go; life went on. I wanted to speak, to make any kind of sound, but nothing. I was having an out-of-body experience, watching the world go by. There were many things I wanted to do, but I was trapped inside my own body. I was locked-in.

When you are locked-in, time goes by so slowly, it just drags by. I don't know how to describe it. It's almost like time stands still. It's a terrible, terrible place to be. It's hard, but you've got to have hope that you are going to get out of this nightmare.

I was at the mercy of other people to care for my every need, and that was incredibly frustrating, but I never lost my alertness. I was completely aware of everything going on around me right from the very start. Thoughts of my life before the stroke—working, reading, friends—and, of course, Kevin kept me going.

My physical therapist moved my limbs in the hope that my brain would relearn how to generate movement. The fear, the loneliness, the indignity, the anxiety of being apart from Kevin and the agony of not moving sufficiently made me terribly sad. In the early days after my stroke, my thoughts were incredibly dark, and I suffered greatly from depression. Kevin visited me six days a week for a few hours each evening; Sunday was his day off. Our time together went quickly, and I was so lonely when he left. I missed all the things couples do that were taken away so abruptly.

I did something almost unheard of, I recovered. I am still recovering, even three years out and counting!

A doctor recently said, "Oh, she's the best outcome I've ever seen after a locked-in. That doesn't mean it's good, but it's the best I've ever seen."[8]

I had my stroke on October 18, 2010. Astonishingly, a little over four months later, I walked out of the MedStar National Rehabilitation Hospital (MNRH), albeit with a walker. It took a lot of work on my part, a great attitude and wonderful doctors, nurses, therapists, friends, and loved ones. I was overwhelmed with joy at being able to move again. Kevin, friends, family, and hospital staff were ecstatic about my recovery and continued with encouragement. Although, I had made amazing progress, it was not enough for me. I am goal-oriented, so I liked being given goals to exceed. For example, if I was supposed to walk fifty feet, I would walk seventy-five feet.

Research in the American Academy of Neurology Journal suggests that despite there being an overall decline in the incidence of stroke, strokes are becoming more common at a younger age. In one recent ten-year period, the rate of strokes in Americans younger than fifty-five went up 84 percent among whites and 54 percent among African Americans. One in five strokes now occurs in adults twenty to fifty-five years old—up from one in eight in the mid-1990s. Doctors should pay a lot more attention to these younger patients. They should make sure their blood pressure and cholesterol are under control and work harder to get them to lose weight and stop smoking. Increases in obesity and diabetes are thought to be factors in the rising incidence of young-adult stroke—though not the only ones.[9]

Although I was locked-in, Kevin, Lisa, and Val talked to me to keep my mind stimulated. In ICU, Kevin explained the surgery to me, saying the doctor went through my groin and then through my heart to get to the brain stem in an area called the *pons Varolii* (or just *pons*) to remove the fresh clot. I could feel my hair, so I knew they did not shave my head. Yeah!

At INOVA Fairfax Hospital in Falls Church, Virginia, I was in ICU for about a week and then moved to a step-down ICU on another floor. I shared a room, but since I could not communicate, they sent a nurse to stay with me during the night to ensure I was comfortable and not alone. Good friends, who also happen to be our dentist and his wife, came to visit. They wear scrubs to their office, so when they came to the ICU in their work scrubs, the hospital staff thought they were staff. I thought that was funny. I could not communicate, but I could hear everything.

I had great doctors, one who even changed my contact lenses, which was not easy for either of us. A young lady came from speech therapy, as my mouth was crooked. They wanted to get my tongue moving again and to help me stop drooling.

A sweet lady from Capital Hospice (now Capital Caring) took my case and was instrumental in getting me into MRNH. I was and am a board member for Hospice Cup (a hospice charity sailing regatta) and worked on some of the gala events.

After surgery and without ever meeting me, only from a clinical standpoint and reading my chart, another doctor told Kevin he should start looking for nursing homes. Because of my condition, a rehab hospital was not recommended as you need to do an hour of physical therapy, an hour of occupational therapy, and an hour of speech therapy, which he thought was beyond my capabilities in my current state.

Kevin said that was *"not acceptable."* If that was the therapy I needed, then that's what I should get. He realized everything I needed to recover was going to be a battle. Nancy and Brian would create red wristbands with this message: "Not Acceptable." And this became our mantra and would be worn by many in support. Rehabilitation is extremely important in the early days and beyond: you don't get that in a nursing home. All a nursing home does is comfort you. I understand doctors cannot promise anything, but they don't fully understand a younger person's needs. Kevin and a caseworker started working to get me into the MNRH.

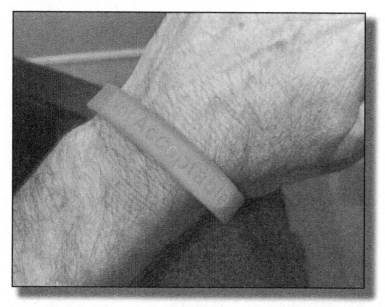

Wristband
November 2010

We vowed to return one day to INOVA Fairfax Hospital and show that doctor he was wrong with his diagnosis. And we did! I went back on my one-year anniversary. Everyone was so happy to see me, saying they preferred me "upright." The doctor in question was in shock at my progress but so happy for my improvement and determination.

My friend Darin set up a CaringBridge website. CaringBridge.com is a charitable nonprofit organization that offers free, personalized websites to people facing serious medical conditions, hospitalizations, or recovery periods. This service allows family members and friends to post and receive consistent information via a single website, eliminating the need to place and receive numerous telephone calls. Visitors can read updates on the patient's condition and post their own messages of support and encouragement to the patient and family.

Kevin liked reading everyone's kind words and prayers. He would also read them to me as I was going through my extensive therapy. I was overwhelmed with so many people's inspirational comments. News spread fast and I heard from people I had not heard from in years, with loving thoughts, prayers, and good wishes. This was a huge help to all of us.

Rehabilitation

People had told Kevin that picking a rehab facility was very important, but it's even more important to be near people you care about, friends and family.

On October 30, 2010, barely two weeks after my first symptoms, I was transported by ambulance to the MedStar National Rehabilitation Hospital in Washington, DC, to begin the long process of preparing to go home. I no longer needed to be in the ICU, but still required a lot of nursing help, rehab, and twenty-four-hour attention. I was still locked-in.

Remember, upon arriving at MNRH all I could do was blink my eyes. Kevin and Lisa were there to meet me. I was scared; I had never been in the hospital for any length of time, much less so sick and unable to move or communicate. The transport company was great, but they were also afraid, as I was so fragile.

MNRH has been operating since 1986, building a top-quality postacute-care (i.e., rehabilitation) facility for adults and children. It has 137 beds and is ranked by physicians in the *U.S. News & World Report* as one of "America's Best Hospitals" for Rehabilitation.

Each year, 800,000 people in the United States suffer a stroke—it's one of the leading causes of disability in the nation.[10] The Stroke Recovery Program at MNRH is one of the largest in the region and the most advanced program of its type in the region. It has been designated as a CARF (Commission on Accreditation of Rehabilitation Facilities)— an accredited specialty program for stroke. Thousands of patients have been treated in the Stroke Recovery Program, and have returned to their families and communities with outcomes that exceed most national benchmarks.[11]

My arrival at MNRH was scary because I had no control and was unsure of what to expect. I shared a room, and my bed was by the door, not near the window. I had no sunlight and was trapped in my own body. The room was dreary and smelled like a hospital. I didn't feel good vibes from the nurse who checked me in, and neither did Lisa or Kevin. Lisa cried, as she did not want me there. It was a nightmare.

But I had wonderful doctors. Doctors Conroy and Maddox thoroughly reviewed my case upon arrival. Dr. Conroy is a specialist in physical medicine and rehabilitation, with a special interest in *neurorehabilitation*. He is the medical director of the Stroke Recovery Program and chief medical information officer, and Dr. Maddox was a resident at the time. Seeing someone in a locked-in state is very rare. They took a chance with me, though I was so sick, and believed an aggressive, acute therapy program would help me improve and thrive.

Dr. Maddox was very inspirational to me and a great motivator in my recovery. She, herself, had lost her leg to a debilitating nerve injury several years before. "You get frustrated sometimes when you can't do things you used to; you know, it takes you extra effort to do certain things," she said. "You always hear the phrase, 'You can do anything you want,' but it depends on the amount of effort that you have to put into it, and sometimes you just don't feel like doing it."

During your first full day at MNRH, you are also evaluated by the different therapists. That day, they were dressed in Halloween costumes; one as a Yahtzee cube. When I saw them, I thought that I had gone crazy. It was a bit confusing, because I had forgotten that it was Halloween. Somebody explained, and I remembered how I used to love Halloween—the costumes, the candy, especially candy corn (!), the trick-or-treaters ...

It turned out this was not going to be my final room. A day or two later, I got pneumonia, which is common in LIS patients. The nurse I had was great and saw the spike in my temperature. I was transferred immediately to MedStar Washington Hospital Center (MWHC) nearby, which is part of the medical complex. I was transported in the underground tunnel to the hospital and left to wait in the emergency room corridor. I thought that they would forget about me. I was alone and felt isolated and scared. I watched the machines, as it was all I could do. I knew that Kevin would come looking for me and that gave me hope. He went to my room at MNRH, and I was gone. He immediately thought the worse. Eventually, he found me over at MWHC.

Two days later, I was transferred to another room at MWHC for continued recovery before going back to MNRH. Two sweet nursing students from MedStar Georgetown University Hospital came and washed my hair. It felt so good to have my hair washed. They would later come to visit me on their own whenever they were at MWHC. This meant so much to me, being cared for and my situation appreciated.

I was delirious watching the drip from the IVs. In my mind, the drip reminded me of a little Chinese man. I wondered what it meant. I was thinking how I could get up and walk out the door; it seemed like such a good idea. I would take the IVs with me after all. But there was nothing I could do. I just lay in the bed staring at the monitors and drips.

A few days later, I was transferred back to MNRH. Room 218 became my home for the next four months.

The nurses' station was close to my room in order for them to quickly respond to my needs, but if my favorites weren't working, I was never sure how closely they were paying attention. There was a picture with glass by the room door. I would look to see who was coming in the room through the reflection, so I was not surprised.

I was alone in my room with absolutely no movement. All my nurses, doctors, friends, and family continued to wear the Not Acceptable bands at MNRH. We didn't take them off until I left rehab over four months later. In the early days, I slept a lot. Your brain needs lots of rest as you go through a trauma. The feeling of helplessness is also hard to take.

The remote that comes with your hospital bed regulates the TV, bed position, the nurses' call button, etc., but it was of no use to me. I couldn't move and had no pressure in my fingertips. The engineering team rigged up an electronic button for me to communicate with my nurses. The bendable arm with a button at the end was put near my head, and I would tap the button with my head, so the nurses' call-button light would come on when I needed them. If the night nurse forgot to position the arm of the bell by my head, Helen (my day nurse) would get very angry. I slept on my back, unable to turn on my side. When I started to move ever so slightly, about five weeks later, our friend Brian showed me that I could adjust the arm myself to be nearer to my head, so this was no longer a problem. Moving felt amazing although the road ahead was still long.

You take little things for granted. Kevin would come in the evening, and we would watch the seven p.m. *Nightly News* together. Then he would leave, and the TV would be on all night as I didn't have the fingertip pressure or arm movement to turn it off.

My days at MNRH started at 6:30 a.m., when Helen (my nurse) and Bea (my tech) came in. Helen is from Nigeria, and Bea is from Trinidad. They became my best friends. They took excellent care of me and referred to me as "their baby." I had to relearn everything, and they helped me. I had a special bed, which moved continuously to allow for alternating pressure. As I could not move, I did not have to be turned every few hours as this bed's continued motion prevented bed sores.

I would get my daily schedule every morning, which included an hour of speech, an hour of occupational, and an hour of physical therapy, plus a half hour of stretching. The head of the wing, Amelia, and Josephine would come by each morning and pray with me for my recovery. They would present weekly goals that I needed to achieve, and they were tacked on a cork bulletin board near the communications board in my room so I could see.

I was given a sponge bath each day (showers and shampooing were once or twice a week with the occupational therapist), and then I was dressed. Solid-colored tops, elastic-waist pants or shorts, socks, and sneakers were now my daily outfits. It felt great to be dressed and out of the hospital gown. My mouth was washed out with flavored swabs—little pieces of foam on a stick that come in a variety of flavors.

At shift change, a couple times a day, the nurse or tech would come and take my blood pressure and temperature. I could hear the machine, which was on a rolling cart, coming down the hall and knew what time it was.

On the weekends or when Bea was off, I would get upset if no one came in the morning and I was not ready for the therapist. It was not my fault, as I was dependent upon everyone, but I didn't like it. This became known and did not happen very often.

Each morning, I would get my medicine, vitamins, and nutrition drink mixed into my feeding tube, plus a shot in my stomach to prevent blood clots from not moving a lot. Sometimes, I would laugh (uncontrollable laughing and crying are part of the stroke), and the feeding tube syringe bubbled over. I got scolded for this, and my laughing, which was contagious, would make my feeding longer than expected. This was a problem because there were other patients to tend to as well.

Once on the weekend, the vitamins wouldn't go through the syringe easily; the nurse pushed the syringe, and I laughed so hard that the fluid sprayed up and onto the ceiling. Both Joan, my weekend nurse, and I learned our lesson, although we all had a good laugh!

Word of my stroke spread through our neighborhood, and all the neighbors signed an oversized Get-Well card. Mary, my boss from Nextel, lives nearby and delivered the card and coordinated dinners to be delivered to Kevin. You really don't know what you need, although people want to help, and they found all kinds of ways to help ease our burdens.

One night, Helen was working the late shift and asked if I was comfortable. She propped the pillows, raised my arm on a pillow, covered me, and put on my foot-drop splint (a.k.a. bunny boot). This warm boot is used to keep the ankle at ninety degrees and prevent the foot from dropping toward the ground. Helen tried so hard to understand me and do everything, but I was just not comfortable. She called in Bea to help and used the communications board. Going through the spelling process, we finally got to the word *pony*. The word I was trying to communicate was determined to be *ponytail*, as my hair was in a ponytail and I could not lay flat; it needed to be removed. That became a joke. Something so simple … was a process.

I was fed five times a day through the feeding tube, and my trachea was cleaned every morning. Tracheostomy suctioning removes the thick mucus and secretions from the trachea and lower airway that you are not able to clear by coughing. Suctioning is done when you wake up in the morning. Cleaning around your trachea tube is the best way to prevent skin breakdown. Nurses would clean around the area with cotton-tipped swabs using mild soap and water or saline. By daily cleaning, your trachea is moist and free from crust. But I disliked the trachea cleaning and hated the suctioning to remove the phlegm. The feeding five times per day was more than I was used to, so I asked for the frequency to be reduced to four; they agreed.

In the early days at MNRH I was tan, having just been to Florida. One weekend, my nurse jokingly said, "You are the tannest white girl I have ever seen"; that made me laugh. By February, my tan had faded, and she said it was a sign "it was time for me to go …" I couldn't have agreed more.

The appearance of the room, so dreary in the beginning, was also addressed. My friend Darin took vivid pictures of flowers and made me a bright, beautiful collage. It made the room so much more cheerful. I also had a big mural on the wall made by Lisa's daughters and their friends. There was a picture of Kevin and me in Bora Bora, and other pictures of friends and family were posted. These pictures gave me motivation to beat this stroke. Get-Well cards were put on the window sill. One week prior, for my birthday and our anniversary, Kevin had gotten me a navy 2011 Jeep Grand Cherokee. I had only driven it a handful of times, so a full-page Jeep newspaper ad was posted with a bow. I looked at all these pictures and daydreamed of normalcy: walking, driving, travel, working, and just doing mundane things with Kevin.

I never had a roommate because of the size and type of apparatus needed to get me out of bed in the beginning. It was like a sack that lifted me up and transferred me into a wheelchair. They call it a Hoyer lift, and you need to be trained in its use. That was eventually removed, and I progressed to sliding along a flat board to move from the bed into the wheelchair or just being lifted to get in and out of bed. An extra bed was always available in the room for other potential patients, but it was not needed.

⊲◦▻

About six weeks after arriving, my doctor said the trachea tube would be removed soon. This was a sign of progress, as I was now able to breathe on my own. The nurses would plug the trachea hole to ensure my oxygen and breathing were good when speaking. But when I would laugh or cough, it would pop out the plug. Another doctor came a few times a week to help me practice speaking while plugged, saying, "One, two, three," which was difficult for me. I tried, but all that came out was a whisper. When I was strong enough, Dr. Maddox and Dr. Conroy came by and removed the trachea tube while I was lying down in bed. *Poof*—it was gone! The doctors checked the area daily and were happy with the progress. The hole closed quickly, and now I just have a small scar on my neck.

As my body was out of whack from the stroke, I was hot all the time. They kept a fan on me, and the nurses would wear sweaters when they came in. I had the room temperature low too. It was winter, and I only slept with a sheet as my cover, never the blanket.

The gym at MNRH is huge, about 6,500 square feet, with high ceilings and fluorescent lights. It's on both the second and third floors and is filled with people dealing with their disabilities. There were people with every imaginable disability—amputees, traumatic brain injury, spinal cord injury, and stroke patients, to name a few. People were trying to walk, learning to rollover, playing games to stimulate their minds, or trying to sit up for the first time, and more. Sometimes you'd hear cheering and clapping when someone made a little progress or had a breakthrough.

My physical therapist, Stacy, and her student at the time, Cierra, tried to give me an electric wheelchair, but I was adamant I was going to walk. I cried and never got used to it. I was told it was just a tool, but to me it was a sign of being disabled. I was told by many to use it to get to therapy on my own and especially Wednesday night when there was bingo.

The first thing I learned was to keep my head up. Boy, your head is heavy! I had to sit in the wheelchair, holding up my head. Each day, the sitting got longer. I would tilt and recline the wheelchair every hour to provide pressure relief.

About five weeks after arriving, I progressed to a tilt table during physical therapy. It is a device that allows you to stand, with your legs and feet supporting full body weight. You are securely strapped in at the knees, waist, and chest. The therapist gradually turns the handle that elevates one end of the table. You proceed slowly, because if you go too fast, your blood pressure drops dramatically and you'll pass out. It takes about fifteen minutes to reach the top, which is at an incline of about 70 degrees.

My physical therapist also had me use a stationary bike with a TENS (transcutaneous electrical nerve stimulation) unit hooked to my thighs and calves to help awaken the muscles. We did this on my right arm also, as this was my weaker side.

Then I progressed to the Zero-G. Based on astronaut training, it is the world's first over-ground body-weight support system—and is now being used at MNRH to treat patients who have had a stroke. It allows patients with amputations or neurological injuries to safely practice walking and navigating obstacles such as stairs or uneven terrain. You are completely supported by a strap-and-trolley system, yet free to move.

As you do, the trolley automatically moves forward or back, staying above you, so that you gradually learn to support more of your weight, without putting pressure on your legs. It helps you regain strength and stability.

These are just a few of the wonderful physical therapy devices I used. Of course, there were mats, parallel bars, stairs, bikes, other machines too.

My arms and legs were stretched each week day by a PT aide. He would come at nine a.m., and we would watch CNN together while he did his job. Later, I also practiced using the walker with him.

Almost twelve weeks later, when I was continent and after the trachea and feeding tubes were removed and those areas had healed, I started pool therapy, which became a luxury I looked forward to. The rectangle, four- to five-foot-deep pool allows for three patients plus their therapists to engage in aquatic therapy. It is a warm and inviting pool where the water is heated to a soothing ninety-two degrees. There is a railing in the middle with a step separating the two water levels. There is also a chair that lowers you into the pool, depending on your needs. I used the chair once and progressed to the entry steps, holding on tightly to the railings.

Pool therapy is ideal for people with arthritis, back injuries, fractures, or anyone with weight-bearing issues. One benefit of aquatic therapy is the buoyancy provided by the water. While submerged in water, buoyancy assists in supporting the weight of the patient. This decreases the amount of weight bearing, which reduces the force of stress placed on the joints. I still do pool therapy twice a week with an aquatic, stroke therapist. It's pure heaven!

It took awhile, but my brain was finally able to make a connection with most muscles. Nerves are damaged in a stroke, and new pathways need to be found, new ways to stimulate the muscles. I am still healing. Repetition in motor usage is important in order for the brain to regain memory of that movement.

I remember showing the doctors, staff, Kevin, and visitors my daily progress, including any new movement. My left side came back first, as I am left-handed, and I could start to envision getting back to my life. But my right side remains weak and a constant challenge.

I worked daily with my speech therapist, Lauren, on my swallowing and speech and then more speech with Kevin in the evening. I practiced with him saying "I love you." Before I could talk again, communicating was like charades, using the communications board and our hands. The first Saturday in December, Lisa stayed over, and I screamed, "I love you!" All the nurses came running with big smiles. I didn't know how to control my volume. It did not hurt; rather, it was exhilarating! Kevin and Lisa debated over who the "I love you" was meant for; they knew it was for both. We had a great evening and watched many episodes of *48 Hours Mystery*.

Luckily, I do not have aphasia. Aphasia is a disorder caused by damage to the parts of the brain that control language. It can make it hard for you to read, write, and say what you mean to say. It is very common in adults who have had a stroke. My memory is intact. The brain is amazing. All words and my speaking came back in full swing. I understand everything and speak just as I did before the stroke. I do play brain teaser games and Scrabble and use the computer and more to keep my mind sharp.

Brian, the janitor in the MNRH housekeeping group, came each day to clean my room. He always said hello and spoke to me knowing I could not respond. He was very sweet. One day he looked out my room window and said, "It looks like it's snowing."

I said, "Yes, but I don't think it will stick."

He looked around the room, not knowing where that came from. When he saw it was me speaking, he ran out of the room to the nurses' station and shouted, "Room 218 is talking! Room 218 is talking!"

They laughed, explaining that they knew and he was correct. He came back in and spoke with me each day. I didn't realize I had touched so many people.

Movement came slowly to me but quickly to the doctors. I had weekly goals for all therapies. My occupational therapist (OT), Kristen, would give me a shower, teach me to dress and to do daily living activities (i.e., brushing your hair, washing your face, brushing your teeth, etc.). Occupational therapy also took place in the gym. We practiced opening and closing all types of jars and bottles, played games, and did individual therapies as well. MNRH has an Independence Square layout on the first floor that simulates real-life scenarios. It includes a bedroom, bath, kitchen, grocery store, diner, bank with ATM, and business center. OTs use the kitchen area to improve patients' abilities to eat and cook, while PTs use the ramps and putting green to help patients regain mobility and strength. Yes, golf therapy! There is also a car in Independence Square to relearn how to get in and out of a car safely, and it measures stopping seconds during driving rehab. Eventually, I progressed to both individual and group activities for occupational and speech therapies.

The group activities were nice. We played games, and it was good to meet other people of all ages going through similar healing processes. We had to use our weak arm and hand when playing games or using equipment. Forcing you to use the affected arm or leg can help improve its function. There was a guy who had been electrocuted, burned, and lost a leg; another who was an Ecuadorian policeman who had taken a bullet for his president; a lady who had MS; and a young man who'd had three strokes and was on dialysis. What you learn is age, race, status, and money make no difference: strokes and other illnesses or major accidents do not discriminate.

The days were tolerable, but the nights were awful. I'd drift off, then wake up. I'd try to go back to sleep, but I couldn't, and those disturbing thoughts would creep in. I would think what if I didn't get better and this was it. What if I couldn't drive again, go out with Kevin, travel, go out with girlfriends … normal things? Would Kevin now be my caregiver, rather than my husband? I missed him terribly and had a hard time getting to sleep, so they had given me medicine to allow me to get some rest.

The medication did not impact my alertness or therapy. I always pushed my therapists to do more. People who came to visit could see my weekly progress. I never wanted to give up; I knew I had not plateaued and would still continue to improve.

I also had a neuropsychologist, Dawn, assigned to me. Neuropsychologists have at least a PhD in psychology and then have furthered their education to include study of the brain and how it affects behavior. Dawn was new to MNRH, and I liked her right away. She would come every day to talk. She asked me what time was the worst—after Kevin would leave for the evening—and so that's when she came. I cried a lot. She would read James Patterson thrillers to me (a favorite), going to the library on her own and signing out the book. I could be transported into the book for a short time.

My moods were like being on a rollercoaster ride. There were moments when I would feel grateful I had not died and appreciative for my daily visitors. Then at night, when Kevin left, I was very sad. I was alone in my room in this hospital bed. I tried to be strong for him, but I cried a lot. Kevin said, "We should buy stock in Kleenex." Your emotions are uncontrollable. I have always been emotional—I cried at commercials, never mind touching stories and the like— but these were out-of-control bursts of sadness, crying, or laughing.

It was a symptom of my stroke and is very common. According to the National Stroke Association, it is called the Pseudobulbar affect (PBA).

> [PBA] is a medical condition characterized by sudden and uncontrollable episodes of crying or laughing. It is sometimes referred to as *emotional liability, pathological crying and laughing,* or *emotional incontinence.* An episode of PBA can occur at any time, even in inappropriate social situations.
>
> PBA is triggered by damage to areas of the brain during a stroke. It is thought to affect more than one million people in the United States with neurologic conditions like

stroke, traumatic brain injury, amyotrophic lateral sclerosis (ALS or Lou Gehrig's disease), Parkinson's disease, and dementias including Alzheimer's disease. PBA is often mistaken for depression, causing it to be underdiagnosed, undertreated, and sometimes inappropriately treated. ...[12]

Sudden and often inappropriate outbursts of PBA can make people feel like their internal emotions and external expressions are disconnected. This can be frustrating for both stroke survivors and their loved ones. ... Learning about PBA is the first step to reclaiming confidence and improving relationships.[13]

I was happy to learn about PBA, as there was now a reason for my emotional outbursts. Also learning that it was a common characteristic was helpful for me, Kevin, and everyone involved. I assumed there was medication to treat it if it was that common. I did feel genuinely sad, though, for everything that had been taken away.

The doctors visited each day and, in December, determined I was no longer locked-in—music to our ears! Everyone was ecstatic. One more step in my progress.

We had a "family" meeting, where all my doctors, nurses, and therapists get together with your family to talk about your status and progress. The feedback was excellent. Dr. Conroy said I was unusual, and we all laughed. This was even written in my discharge papers. Good friends of ours,

John (who is in the medical industry) and Cheri, came from Marblehead to be at the meeting as our advocates. It was most helpful, and we appreciated them being there.

Other good friends, Buzz and Suzanne from Marblehead, also visited. We greatly appreciated their visit, care, and concern too. They spread the word of my progress to the old neighborhood.

My therapists told my nurses that I had to start using the wheelchair to go to my therapies and other activities *without help.*

I looked forward to bingo, which was on Wednesday evenings, and I would attend starting in January. It was a nice activity put on by the Junior League of Washington, DC. Winners could choose from small gifts. It was held in the gym, and I had to get there by wheelchair. I hadn't practiced a lot with the wheelchair, and the door strip that was between the hardwood floors in my room and the carpeted hallway outside was tricky. I wheeled myself right into the trash bins that were in the hall on the right, against the wall. Bea laughed and asked Helen if she knew what her patient was doing? Kevin would visit on these days, and I would already be in the gym. He was happy I was out of my room.

MNRH has a beautiful outdoor area with a sculpture. Much to the disappointment of my therapists and visitors, I would not go outside for my four-month stay, as I did not want to be in the wheelchair. I missed fresh air, but I was stubborn.

Some days I found MNRH a warm and friendly place where I would get better. Other days, it felt like a prison where I had been condemned to an indefinite sentence. *Why me?* I thought.

In early February, I was told that I was now where most typical stroke patients are when they arrive; that was great to hear. I realized I'd have to leave MNRH at some point. The doctor came each day, still amazed with my progress, and suddenly announced I would be going home soon. I could not believe it; I was going home and would be in my own surroundings and with Kevin.

Before discharge, however, you are allowed a Day Pass. You have to be back by a certain time (like Cinderella) or you are *automatically* discharged. I went through my house and got familiar with moving around with the walker. I walked up and down the stairs with help and was able to get to the second-floor bedrooms to say hello to my shoes! We also went to a friend's home for a visit and dinner away from the hospital setting. This was a big step for me, and I was very excited to do this. Kevin had undergone some training to ensure that any needs I had throughout the day could be handled. It was very special. We ate a lovely meal in their dining room … just *like real people.*

Kevin and I instituted a date night every Saturday to practice enjoying life as we had before the injury. Our first date was with Lisa and Greg. They brought in food from a favorite Italian restaurant, and we ate and played Scrabble in the MNRH cafeteria. Another date night was with Kevin's sister and my stepdad. Again, we had dinner and played games. We also celebrated Kevin's birthday with a moist, chocolate cake that I shared in, savoring every delicious bite!

February 15, 2011, was the day that had been set by the insurance company to discharge me from MNRH, but my case manager and my doctor convinced them to let me stay an additional two weeks. March 1 became the new targeted release date. Upon release, I would be enrolled in the MNRH Outpatient Day Program, formally called the Transitions Neurological Day Treatment Program, which was five days a week of continued, intense therapy, six hours a day.

Kevin had named my weak right arm Henry and my weak right leg Elvis. He was trying to bring some humor to the situation. We laughed, and Dr. Conroy even referred to "Henry" in my official hospital discharge papers.

Swallowing, Eating, and My Voice

It is not uncommon to have trouble swallowing after a stroke. This is called *dysphagia*. *Aphasia*, on the other hand, is the partial or complete impairment of the ability to communicate resulting from brain injury. A patient's prognosis will greatly depend on several factors, such as the location and extent of the underlying damage. Additional factors of importance are the patient's age, general health, and mental health and motivation.

My memory is great, and my voice is getting stronger, but I still can't carry a tune. Leafy lettuce, corn, peas, etc., still make me cough. In fact, I tend to cough and sneeze everytime I eat!

It was early January and another barium-swallow test was scheduled. I had failed the swallow test in November, still aspirating (going down the wrong pipe). Everyone agrees that was too early, but we had to try. I felt like I had let Kevin down. Lauren and I practiced swallowing techniques each day. Barium sulfate is a metallic compound that shows up on X-rays and is used to help see abnormalities in the esophagus and stomach. When taking the test, you are given different food consistencies (from pudding to Fig Newtons) mixed with barium. This test provides a visual image on screen of these foods as they travel through your mouth and down your throat. It's helpful for diagnosing dysphagia because your doctor can see if there are any problems with how the muscles of your mouth and throat work when you swallow. The entire second-floor staff were so excited and happy for me when I passed the test on January 6, 2011. I had not been allowed to eat or have liquids up to then.

Sometimes Kevin would wet a washcloth in ice cold water, and I would suck on it. That was wonderful as I was so parched. Now I could gradually start eating again, beginning with soft foods. Lauren, my speech therapist, had lunch with me the first day to ensure all went well. The food was pureed, and the drink, a thick consistency, but I didn't care. I had not had anything since mid-October. Eating and chewing felt strange at first. The meal servers would come take my order each day. What a luxury!

I was told if I ate three meals a day, my feeding tube could come out. I ate as requested in order to make this happen. I was also told I was "the neatest eater." Feeding myself came back to me easily, using normal utensils. At first, cutting food was difficult, but it continues to get easier. Practice makes perfect.

It was a snowy day when a doctor came by in order to remove the feeding tube. He asked me to lie down and immediately *yanked the feeding tube out of my stomach*! After that, and a little pain, he left the room. The nurses then attended to the wound it left in my stomach, which closed quickly, and I was no longer *attached*—that is, I didn't have anything in my body that connected me to the hospital. All the medicines, except vitamins, were discontinued because of my progress. The shots continued due to my lack of mobility.

Allison & Dr. Conroy
May 2012

Allison, Helen, Bea
May 2012

Allison, Helen, Bea
May 2012
(All photos: Cal Covert)

The Holidays

Thanksgiving came upon us so soon after I started my recovery at MNRH, and my sister-in-law, Deneen, was coming to visit from Cleveland. She happens to be a respiratory therapist, so her input was extremely helpful. Kevin and Deneen spent Thanksgiving morning with me. We watched *Planes, Trains and Automobiles*, which was a ritual for all of us. After that, they went to my uncle's house in Annapolis, Maryland, for dinner. I was lonely when they left. I had taken my first swallow test earlier in the week and failed. My swallowing muscles were not strong enough yet, and I could not eat on Thanksgiving Day.

A former boss and his wife had a holiday party. They gave all their guests the red "NOT ACCEPTABLE" wristbands and took pictures of everyone wearing them. They sent the pictures to Kevin, who shared them with me. The pictures made me cry, as I was overwhelmed with love, support, and caring.

Christmas was around the corner, so Kevin adorned my room with a decorated wall Christmas tree that Deneen had made and other holiday decorations. You can't have anything on the floor that might take up space or that you might trip over. My neighbor brought a plug-in menorah, which we put on the window sill. The room became very festive.

A few weeks before Christmas, Kevin came on a Saturday and said he was spending the night. He shut the door and told the nurses not to disturb us. I was confused. He said he had something to tell me. He then said those awful words, "Your mom passed away in October."

I did not believe him. How could this be happening? I was the one who was sick! He then told me she passed away one week after my stroke, as a result of her surgery from diverticulitis and, he said, of a broken heart for what happened to me. He had not told me because I was not able to express my feelings. He had wondered why I never asked about her, and I explained, "I was so focused on my recovery and I knew she was also recovering from her major surgery."

The family had the funeral, and she was cremated. And now that I was healing and able to communicate, everyone felt like it was the right time to tell me.

I cried, "No, no, no. This can't be true!" He cried too. He had not wanted to tell me and felt terrible. He spent the night because he did not want me to be alone.

The next day, all the MNRH staff came to pay their condolences. Lou, my aunts and uncles, some friends, and my mom's closest friend, Millie, came by to comfort me. We told amusing stories in her memory, and it was like a celebration. Millie is now my "acting" mom. I have known her since I was seven. Growing up, Millie would frequently join us for dinners, Easter brunch, and other holiday celebrations.

This was the first time Lou had seen me since my stroke. Kevin had kept him from visiting, as he was afraid he might accidentally tell me about my mom's passing. Lou didn't know what to expect in seeing me. Lou was wonderful; I was touched to see him, and we ended up comforting each other.

I guess I have not really dealt with my mom's death, as my recovery has continued to be my priority. I hate to say it, but it was kind of a blessing, as I don't know how I could have dealt with her *and* my therapy. Plus, she and Kevin would have been fighting over what was right for me.

Even before I found out about my mom's passing and when Kevin and others would talk to me, I often looked up at the ceiling and stared intensely. He would ask me what I was looking at and thought maybe I knew about my mom and was looking up at her. I did not know, and I guess I was looking up because when you're just lying in bed, there's not much else to look at.

One Sunday in December, Kevin had a holiday party for me at MNRH. The party was to thank family, staff, and friends who had done so much for us. My friend Nancy made holiday cookies, which we all decorated for the hospital staff. She also brought a homemade gingerbread house, which I decorated by myself. Boy, that was therapy! It's a very tedious process and uses your fine motor skills. I still could not eat, but we served punch, cheese and crackers, and cookies (I did lick a bit of the frosting!). My gingerbread house was displayed on the second-floor nurses' station, and everyone enjoyed it. Photos were taken, and it made the hospital newsletter and the 2011 MNRH calendar. Another patient came by and started eating the candy over the next few days! Everyone got a big laugh out of that.

Kevin spent Christmas night with me. We had our own little Christmas and exchanged gifts. Nancy and Brian came with their kids on Christmas Eve to exchange gifts as well. They bought a Kindle for me to give to Kevin and helped me wrap it. Kevin gave me a Samsung tablet that had game applications to help with my dexterity and stimulate my mind. Lisa and Greg came to visit, and Greg loaded more games on the tablet including Angry Birds, still a favorite of mine.

Kevin bought a Charlie Brown tree and poinsettias for our home to add a little cheer, although neither of us felt much like celebrating. Kevin's sister came in, and my friend Lisa invited Kevin for Christmas dinner. Her nine-year-old daughter, Elizabeth, was his date. To me, once he left in the afternoon, it was just another day. Yet again, I could not eat Christmas dinner.

The next holiday was New Year's; nothing special except Kevin spent the night. Deneen sent a package, which included hats, streamers, and party favors. We shared them with the staff who worked that night. They were very appreciative, and the other patients loved it. We wore the hats and watched the ball drop on TV, just like we always have done.

Sharing the Visits

During my stay, Kevin designated a friend or family member to come and see me each day and that would relieve him from faithfully coming to the hospital — although he did, but Sunday was his day off. Each day I had someone visit me mostly around lunchtime or early evening to encourage me as I went through my therapy. Kevin would take home my clothes twice a week to launder them. Who would believe I missed doing laundry? But I did. I so wanted to do laundry like I had before. Brian and Nancy would come every Friday. Brian would clean my teeth each visit, and Nancy would brush my hair, which was so relaxing. Lisa would come every Sunday; she would style my hair and shave my legs. That's a good friend! Kevin and his sister even colored my hair. That's love. We began calling Kevin, Fabio!

Before my stroke, I ran errands in my town, McLean, Virginia, and was a loyal customer to all. They paid me back in spades. My nail person came to the hospital and gave me a manicure and pedicure; my hairstylist came and cut my hair; and my eye doctor came to change my contact lenses. Even the people at the dry cleaners and grocery store were upset when they learned the news. All this brought some sense of normality, humility, and gratitude, even though I was in the hospital.

My girlfriend Verdery came twice from Atlanta to visit. We had met her and her late husband, Bob, in a bar in Marblehead and became quick friends. We had visited them yearly in Atlanta when Kevin would run the Peachtree Road Race. They moved back to Georgia a year after we met. It was good to see her while I was in the hospital.

A friend of Lisa's from Italy came to visit, and Lisa's parents and in-laws came to the hospital, among others. Kevin was careful about who came to visit and when, always ensuring I was up to seeing them. He was very protective.

The MNRH Day Program and Other Therapies

After being discharged from inpatient treatment, I was enrolled in the outpatient therapy Transitions Neurological Day Treatment Program, which everyone just called the Day program. The program is wonderful, and MNRH is the only facility in the area to offer such a thing. It was six hours a day and included all the therapies, plus cognitive thinking, how to maneuver around the house, cooking, even field trips to help get back into the community. We'd visit different museums and galleries, including the National Geographic Museum and the Basilica of the National Shrine of the Immaculate Conception. We also went bowling, traveling everywhere in the MNRH van. I tried using the escalator during one of the museum visits, but it was too soon, and I was very scared. I graduated from the Day program the day before Memorial Day 2011.

Outpatient therapy three times a week would now begin, but we took a week off. Kevin thought we both deserved a vacation. We went to Naples, Florida, where we had our vacation home. However, I did a lot of therapy in our pool, so no real rest for me. Darryll drove down from Orlando to visit us. It was difficult telling people there my story. It still makes me very sad. Kevin tries to put a positive spin on it, saying I could have died or remained forever in a locked-in condition.

During the early outpatient days, I did an intense five-day-a-week speech program for four weeks. Called LOUD, it was developed for Parkinson's patients, but found to be helpful for stroke patients too. I was informed my left vocal cord was paralyzed and referred to the head of *otolaryngology* (ear, nose, and throat doctor) at George Washington Hospital in Washington, DC. The doctor took a look and said my vocal cord was actually not paralyzed anymore, just very weak. It would only take time to get stronger.

Coughing is common in stroke patients. I have to be very focused when eating or drinking or I can aspirate; it is exhausting and annoying. Dr. Conroy recommended I go to John's Hopkins in Baltimore and have another swallow test. The test showed that I was not aspirating, but I was having some issues. There was a delay in food and drink going down caused by weak muscles in my throat. Again, I was told it would take time and improve as the body continues to heal. Now, it's basically all physical therapy, walking, balance—and time—that's left.

4

Going Home

MARCH 1st FINALLY CAME—MY DISCHARGE DATE—WHICH was over four months after my stroke. Lisa bought me a new outfit for the occasion of going home. The staff threw me a party and let me walk out with my walker, not a wheelchair, which is standard hospital procedure. "It's for moments like these that I joined nursing!" said Helen with a tear in her eye. Bea was off that day, but called in. Another one of my favorites, Joan, came in on her day off.

It was the first time I had been outside in months, and the air was fresh. Spring was around the corner, and I was like a blooming flower. It was wonderful. I was getting into my car … to go to my house … and sleep in my own bed. Wow! During the trip home, I took in all the mundane sights as if it were the first time I had seen them. Everything in the house was just as I had left it. I was home.

My sister-in-law, Deneen, drove from Cleveland to help with my homecoming. They made me take home a wheelchair, but I would never use it. We arranged to have an aide during the week, so Kevin could go to work, and the aide could take me to MNRH for therapy and see to my needs. My stay at MNRH was the longest stay they had had for recovery, second only to a sheik from Saudi Arabia. Insurance would continue to pay, as long as I continued to show progress.

I was introduced to my home-health aide, Treveline, who was also from Trinidad, my first week home. She would come Monday through Friday, 6:30 a.m.–3:30 p.m. She helped me do my exercises in bed, take a shower, get dressed, have breakfast—she would crush my vitamins, and I would take them in applesauce. And then she'd drive me to MNRH.

While I was still using the walker, Kevin, Treveline, and I went to a hospital-sponsored stroke seminar together. We wanted to gather as much information as possible. The speaker was a former Miss America who had had a stroke at a time when there was little-to-no rehabilitation available. She worked alone with inner determination and regained her life and is fine and healthy today. There was a breakout session on driving, which seemed the impossible dream at the time. Seeing others at the seminar who had had strokes made me thankful for my progress and gave me hope for the future.

Treveline had applied for a job at MNRH previously with no response. I introduced her to several people during our therapy trips, giving her a glowing recommendation.

She was eventually offered a full-time position and started at MNRH in July 2011. I was sad to see her go, but thrilled I could help. Again, I am trying to make something good come out of having the stroke. I longed for the days when no aide would be needed. That day has finally arrived, and I treasure my time alone.

Treveline's replacement was Ellen—and she was great too. I was lucky to have had wonderful aides. I found them both through the home-health agency Right at Home, which was referred to us. They became like family. That was lucky, as it was difficult getting used to having someone always there. Being an only child and even as an adult, I was used to time alone, and I loved it. I was used to doing what I wanted, when I wanted … not needing to wait for or depend on someone else to do it. Privacy, and therefore modesty, also goes out the window when you experience a traumatic event such as a stroke.

I have what's called a *Trendelenburg gait*. Named for a German surgeon, it is an abnormal gait caused by weakness of the hip. The Trendelenburg gait mostly occurs when we have to deal with a neuronal injury. A limp is simply the inability to walk normally due to a disease or injury. A Trendelenburg gait results from weakness in the *gluteus medius* muscle. The weakness causes the hip to drop. When walking, a patient with a Trendelenburg gait will lean to the opposite side of the injury to keep the leg from falling. In a healthy person, the two legs carry the weight evenly. When you walk, by necessity, you take one foot off the ground per step and temporarily carry all the weight on one leg. I am working hard to overcome this.

Treveline and then Ellen and I would walk the mall during the week. At first, I used a walker; then I progressed to a four-prong cane. We tried to walk the mall twice around, but I became tired and had to rest along the way. I got down to only one sit-down break for each trip around the mall. Ellen also taught me to use the escalator. Mall patrons were very patient, and I tried not to hold people up.

I had a weekend aide also. Her name was Victoria, from Nigeria, and she too was wonderful. She was studying to become an LPN (licensed practical nurse) and always had a big medical book. She'd come Saturday and Sunday, 9:00 a.m.–4:00 p.m. She'd do the same things as Treveline and Ellen, but since I didn't have the Day program on weekends, she'd also helped me go through all my mom's things. Boy, my mom was a saver. She had old magazines, recipes, papers, clothes, shoes, you name it. We went to her house every Saturday, all day, from March until July. I had the Salvation Army come many times to haul off piles and piles, saving precious memories for myself.

It was wonderful being home and being with my things. Everything was as I'd left it; nothing had changed. There's nothing like coming home. We had a small party on my first Sunday home to thank everyone for their love and support.

I was home but could not do anything. Nor could I fit into anything! I had gotten used to being in elastic pants and had gained weight from the feeding tube and pureed food, while not being mobile. I immediately put myself on a diet and lost over twenty pounds in six to nine months. Everyone thought I was crazy—didn't I have more important things to focus on?—but this was important to me. Kevin bought an elliptical bike, which I continue to use every day for one hour, and I got a treadmill for Christmas 2011.

I went to see my primary doctor, and he too was mystified by my stroke and thrilled with my progress.

I started writing the journal on my CaringBridge site and liked doing it. People were so happy to hear from me. I like reading people's comments, feedback, and well wishes. It was and still is humbling.

5

My New Life

IN MARCH 2012, A YEAR AFTER GETTING OUT OF THE hospital, we went to visit my uncle and his wife in Delaware. We went to dinner at a nearby country club, which happened to be having a dinner for doctors in a separate room. My aunt, who lives about twenty-five minutes away, joined us. Her husband was traveling.

I ordered prime rib, and a piece got caught in my throat. Kevin saw me struggling and starting to turn blue. He did the Heimlich maneuver with no success. I was like a rag doll. My aunt ran into the doctors' dinner yelling, and they came running. The general manager called 911.

The ambulance arrived in minutes, and they put an oxygen mask on me and used tongs to remove the piece of meat. I was immediately stabilized. Kevin explained to them that I had had a stroke, and I was taken to the hospital as a precaution to ensure my throat would not swell up and cause breathing problems. *Not again*, I thought. They did an X-ray to determine if any damage had been done. Thank God it had not. Many times, choking occurs on fish or chicken, which have bones that are more irritating and intrusive. I was discharged a few hours later, and we returned home to my uncle's home.

I was exhausted. My aunt made a wonderful brunch on Sunday though, which consisted of things that were soft!

I learned my lesson and now cut food into very small pieces. Things I used to take for granted are no longer easy, and I do not take risks; I don't want to disrupt my progress.

I graduated from outpatient occupational therapy and started going to the grocery store with my aides and now with Kevin, doing laundry, making the bed, emptying the dishwasher, setting the table, taking a shower, getting dressed, and even changing my contact lenses. Doing small things should be celebrated; they are big to stroke survivors. Walking is still difficult, although I have progressed to a single-point cane or no cane when someone is nearby. I still need to also work on my balance.

In the early days, when Kevin had to go away for a night, we had Victoria, my weekend aide, stay over. Friends bought us baby monitors. One monitor was in the family room and one on the night stand on my side of the bed. This way, I could be heard if I needed anything. Who knew baby monitors could be useful to adults?

Kevin has become more comfortable leaving me alone as time passes. He has even left me for one night to visit a friend in Philly. My neighbors are never far, and we always let them know if he is going to be away. Kevin also has me wearing a monitoring device that can reach out to him, neighbors, and 911 if I fall or require help.

I started OT once a week again to make my right hand stronger and improve my fine motor skills even more, but a few months ago I stopped as I could do the exercises at home. I can put on my jewelry, but necklaces are still hard. I can button, tie, and zip. Therapists find I am more coordinated with my right hand, although I am left-handed. Odd; no one knows why.

My emotions are better too as I take medicine. I still get sad when I think of everything in my life that has changed because of the stroke. I am very sensitive to loud noises as well, and I scare easily.

When I was in the hospital, Kevin had told me he found a nice place for Lou to move to. My uncle had seen it also and agreed. When I was out of the hospital, Kevin took me to see it. I didn't like it and nixed this location. I had an epiphany that we should move Lou to Florida to an Independent-living community. After all, Florida is set up to accommodate seniors, and the weather is accommodating as well. It was a great idea as we had had a second home there and still plan to move there (hopefully soon) for retirement.

Kevin and I went down to see what was available, and we narrowed it down to four facilities. We then brought Lou to Florida to decide for himself. He liked them all; chose one and we moved him down in August 2011. He has a beautiful one-bedroom with a lanai, full kitchen, housekeeping once a week, three meals a day, two pools, lots of activities, and wonderful staff and residents. He is happy, and we visit frequently.

I nominated Helen, my nurse at MNRH, for *Washingtonian Magazine's* Nursing Award, and she won, along with nine other nurses from around the area. I was the only patient to have sent in a nomination. There was a sit-down dinner. Many of the people I worked with and executives from MNRH attended. I was given a standing ovation when recognized for my story. It was also great recognition for the hospital and Helen. Well-deserved.

Allison and Helen
December 2011
(photo: Erik Uecke)

Allison and MRNH Staff
December 2011
(photo: Erik Uecke)

Life continues to improve. I did a paid-research project for a friend and planned my fiftieth birthday, September 2011, in the Bahamas. We see friends on a consistent basis. I am back on the board of Hospice Cup and redesigned the sponsorship brochure with an agency friend. I help Kevin do some marketing and pull weekly reports for his staffing business. I took a presentation skills class at the Stroke Comeback Center in Vienna, Virginia (not far from McLean), and am helping them with some marketing and their ten year anniversary as well. The center is only one of six in the United States. It's wonderful, as everyone who attends has had a stroke and are all in different stages of recovery.

I did a stroke video for MedStar Health, my story was in a philanthropy letter, and raised $2,100 for National Stroke Month in May 2012. I also spoke to the current group during the "coping skills" session at the MNRH Day program.

I was an Honorary Chair at MNRH's 2013 Stroke Lunch and Fashion Show. Three stroke survivors, including me, told our stories at the event. My girlfriend bought a table for the event; I was humbled. The table was for ten guests and included champagne! I had no trouble filling the seats and actually had thirteen girlfriends attend. The luncheon was to raise awareness for "Women and Stroke." We are just average women, and if it can happen to us, it can happen to anyone.

I took the driving rehab program at MNRH. The instructor was very impressed, and no car adjustments are required for me. Lisa was with me during my first class. I got in the car with the instructor, and away I went, leaving Lisa at the curb. It all came back to me. How liberating! Kevin takes me out every weekend to practice my driving and retaught me to parallel park. We drive in my Jeep, and turning the wheel is hard, even though it's power steering. In September 2012, I was approved by the DMV with no restrictions or modifications. I don't drive alone, though, as my walking on uneven surfaces is not great, but I am working on it. Once you drive to your destination, you have to walk!

Allison driving
May 2012
(photo: Cal Covert)

Personal trainers having experience working with stroke patients were recommended by my physical therapists at MNRH and Sibley Memorial Hospital. I interviewed them and started working with Jonathan in September 2012. My goals are strength, stamina, balance, and walking. He sees much improvement since we began and more on the horizon.

I have been doing pool therapy with an aquatic stroke therapist, Cheryl, twice a week for two plus years at Sibley Memorial Hospital in DC. That hospital is much closer to my home. There is a pool-exercise class of older women before my individual therapy, and the women have sort of adopted me. They give me encouragement and always have a smile. One sweet lady even came to the MNRH Stroke Lunch and sat at my table with all my other friends; I was touched.

I did an all-day neuropsychological (cognitive) exam at MNRH. They take the results and cross-reference against someone of similar age and background to see what percentile I fall in. They also use it as a baseline, as they did not know me before my stroke. I signed up for Brain HQ to keep my mind stimulated. Kevin and I also play Scrabble (I still win!), Word Up, and Word Search, and other games and puzzles on my tablet.

We are no longer able to travel at the spur of the moment. We need to book a wheelchair at the airport to get to and from the plane. We also need a handicap room at hotels. These rooms have grab bars in the bath/shower and toilet area and usually a seat in the shower, or we use a separate shower bench. We have found people very accommodating and helpful. I long for the day when I can walk through the airport without planning it.

I still have trouble telling my story and have sad times. I know I am lucky and had an amazing recovery. I have a wonderful husband, amazing friends, and great therapists. Our twenty-second anniversary was in October 2013, and I am happy to be here.

Things can change in a minute, so enjoy your life each and every day to the fullest.

I thank everyone at MNRH; they are gifts.

I hope you found this book inspirational and helpful, God forbid this happens to you or a loved one.

To the medical community: don't give up on young stroke patients by sending them to a nursing home. Acute rehabilitation is so important in recovery. We have a life ahead. Give us the chance and the tools to get better and get our life back. Try to give families some sense of hope, but of course, be truthful and realistic.

To family and friends: thank you for your love, continued support, and encouragement; may other survivors be so lucky. Sometimes, family and friends are scared. You don't know what to expect or do. I just wanted to be loved for who I was then, and now, and I found being around you so important to my overall state. Your ongoing encouragement was and is so welcome and appreciated.

To my fellow stroke survivors: continue to fight the fight and know you are not alone. Be the best you can be, and never give up hope and never stop improving. Don't compare yourself to other survivors, as everyone is different. If it helps, connect with other survivors and share your story; it is therapeutic. There is a lot of information and many associations available with invaluable materials and assistance. Don't be afraid to ask for help, but also try to do things safely on your own when someone is nearby and spotting you. You don't realize what you can do. Remember, you've taken the first step in that you survived, and you have your whole life ahead.

> *Anger, denial, and great rehabilitation are key motivators to stroke recovery in the early days. Early acceptance of a bleak prognosis—both by the survivor and health professionals—is more likely to leave an individual the way they are.*[14]
>
> —Kate Allatt, 2012
> Stroke survivor and author of
> *Running Free* and *Gonna Fly Now*
> Winner of Extraordinary Woman of Year 2011
> 2012 Finalist - Yorkshire Woman of Achievement Awards
> Founder of her *fighting strokes.org* charity

6

CaringBridge Guestbook

BELOW ARE SOME MOTIVATING AND TOUCHING COMMENTS from the guestbook on my CaringBridge site.

The messages are shown in order from today through the stroke date.

> *I know you know by now that "slow and sure wins the race," and your positive attitude is so important in continuing the progress. Recognize and celebrate each and every move forward as you continue to do. We are so happy to continue to hear these reports of continuing improvement.*

> *Your "back to business" comment cracks me up, but it is also why you are improving so dramatically. Keep up the good work.*

We still can't believe just how amazing you truly are! It was two years ago this month when we first saw you after your stroke. It was so heartbreaking seeing you in such a helpless state, so unlike our incredibly strong friend. But now look at you, girlfriend! So happy that you can inspire and give hope to other stroke patients who may feel frightened that they will never recover. Watching you drive your car should give hope to everyone! You are just the most inspiring role model, not just for stroke patients but for everyone.

You're amazing ... driving! Your strength and determination has touched so many including my mom, who you know recently had a stroke. The support and guidance you and Kevin provided to me have helped focus her recovery so much that she is exceeding every goal they set for her.

Keep pushing yourself and others, it is this amazing power that touches so many lives.

You inspire and amaze me with every accomplishment!

You continue to amaze me. Your inner strength and determination also continues to lift me up when I think the going gets rough. You will always and forever be the most influential inspiration in my life. I think of you daily—your bracelets on my door knobs keep your presence all throughout my house—but I wouldn't need the bracelets to make me think of you!—they are like a symbol of faith and believing ... in oneself and others.

We're much older than you are my dear, but I'm not sure that I would ever be as brave as you have been throughout this long road to recovery. And recovering is surely what you are doing with grace and dignity.

So thrilled to hear that you continue to make such great progress ... what an incredible journey you have been on, and your perseverance and success are an inspiration to all of us!

March first will indeed be a day to celebrate your incredible achievement and a testimony to your fighting spirit. A good role model for all of us, no matter our age!

I loved seeing that you are helping other stroke patients get through similar situations. It's an amazing gift for them to have you and your successes to give them hope and support.

It's so hard to believe that it was a year ago that Buzz and I were sitting in your kitchen with Kevin and Deneen and we were all crying because we were so afraid of what your prognosis was going to be. Now I look back at that day and think how foolish we were to ever question your incredible determination and fighting spirit. You are the ultimate comeback kid, and we couldn't *be more proud of you. I'm sure you just want to wipe this past year off the map, but we are just so happy that we have you back, and now your beautiful voice is coming back too! Woo-hoo!*

I am so inspired by your hard work and progress—you've become my modern hero and you are an invaluable role model for those of us with little aches and pains.

We are so happy that you continue to be our #1 miracle. The sky is the limit, Ali, and nobody can ever bet against you!

So glad to see you're making progress—very exciting! Also, your thought, "But you have to take risks and push yourself forward!" was very inspiring and just what I needed today. Thanks, and keep pushing yourself forward!

We continue to marvel at all the activities you are getting back into while continuing to make incredible progress. Getting back into the swing of things that brought you joy and fulfillment in the past will most certainly speed up progress even more in the present and future.

You are the fighter we always knew you to be—the miracle of your recovery comes from within you. As we like to say—there's no quit in that girl. We are so very excited and so happy with your progress, and thrilled (but not surprised) to be able to watch and hear about it.

Zippy! What a great nickname. Thank you for teaching us so much about courage and determination. You are an amazing inspiration.

It's so great to hear of our continued progress and the amazing accomplishments. You are a wonderful inspiration.

The change of seasons makes me think how amazing your strength is and how every week you just surpass all the obstacles as if they are nothing—with your sheer determination and strength. You keep me so grounded in focusing on what really matters. Thank you for that.

We are so happy for your continued recovery, and yes, you are getting your life back, one day at a time. Your strength and determination should be bottled and sold to all who lack faith.

Al, you're back again!

You're a total rock star! I'm so happy to hear that things are on the up and up. What a role model you are to everyone for your strength, determination, and positivity.

We love you. Miracles do happen.

You are a lesson in perseverance and positive thinking and never giving up, for all of us. So many things we take for granted, Allison, and you have taught us that everything we have is a blessing. I cry seeing how hard you fight to come back from a very, very hard challenge that would normally have wiped out anybody's willpower and well-being. Sharing your story and what you went through is something the whole world can learn from.

You have always inspired me with your hard work, focus, and dedication in the workplace, and now to see your hard work, focus, and dedication toward recovery is not only inspiring ... it—and you—are awe-inspiring!!!

We're so pleased and proud of the progress you've made, which is nothing short of a miracle! Our prayers for you and Kevin have been answered.

You and Kevin are both truly remarkable! Allison, eating and drinking, how amazing is that! You are living proof that miracles do happen every day!

You are a true inspiration. I know how much you look forward to returning home and it is a well-deserved triumph.

Keep up the hard work and imagine a big crowd of people cheering you on. You inspire me to do more!

You are so amazing. You are Super Woman ... literally, the superhero comes to my mind every time I think of you. I'm inspired by your strength and determination. Each of your victories, large and small, are victories we all celebrate.

You have blown me away with your progress and your tenacity to beat this! I always knew you were amazing but even you have trumped yourself. Keep up the hard work. ...

Amazing grace, precious friend. We can't even begin to express how happy we are that the feeding tube is gone. Keep answering our prayers and being our #1 miracle.

Keep pushing hard. We are all there cheering you on! :)

There was never any question in our minds that you would walk and talk again. We know you are a very purposeful young lady—who does not know the word quit. We are very proud of who you are, and so very proud of your abilities to accomplish whatever you set your sights on! Keep up the amazing work you are doing to heal yourself—we know you will achieve all that you set your sights on!

I think I have a new hero! Your energy, drive, and accomplishments ... wow. Keep it up!

Wow, was I shocked to see that walker in your room, and the fact that you are using it makes me smile inside. You are and will always continue to be an inspiration to anyone who has ever met you. I don't have to remind you to keep up the good work, as all of your nurses have agreed they have a hard time keeping up with you.

It was so great getting your phone call the other night. Your voice is just so strong and clear. I still get chills thinking about the incredible obstacles you have faced these past few months and how you have managed to overcome them with sheer determination and incredibly hard work. The doctors' mouths at NRH must be hanging open all the time seeing what new tricks you come up with every day. You are both inspirations to all of us. Your devotion, love and strength make my vote for the dynamic duo, and you continue to stay in our thoughts and prayers every day!

You, my friend, are amazing! WOW. I cannot imagine how hard you are working every day to have made the progress that you have. Your strong will and determination of Not Acceptable is paying huge dividends. You have become an inspiration to so many people!! You have become my rock.

The girls talk about you every day, and we review your progress on this wonderful site. It has been such a lesson for them (and me) to see how you are a fighter and are so absolutely amazing. We are so thankful you are making such progress and understand you are pushing yourself by working extra hard to make these amazing goals. We are proud of you and are proud of the example you can provide for us all.

We are literally overjoyed and so happy at the progress you have made ...and that's because you're a fighter! Just shows that the docs don't really know that much ... You are rewriting the rules to achieve success that medicine alone cannot do, and we've very proud of you.

If I were a betting woman, my money would be on you! I am so thrilled and inspired by all of the progress you have made to date and will continue to make! Your spunk and tenacity have always been, and will always be a thing of wonder to me.

Your progress is amazing, just like you. We are all proud to wear the red wristbands as Allison's army. Not Acceptable is right. Take care of yourself and continue to fight hard every day. We love you,

---

Once an over achiever, always an overachiever! So glad to hear (and not at all surprised) that you are blowing away the benchmarks that your team has set for you. Way to go! Sounds like you've got a great group of people working with you to put the best plan together for your recovery.

So Allison, apparently the doctors, et al, say you are "unusual." Why didn't they just ask us? We would have told them.

I am so proud of you! Your strength and determination are extremely impressive. You are my hero!!!

You are totally stumping the medical community with your amazing progress, but no one who knows you is really surprised. You are made of true grit and determination and keep showing everyone what you're made of, because it is definitely paying off!

We had a gathering this weekend of several of your friends, and we all passed around red wristbands for support. "Not acceptable" is a great motto to live by, and we are sending positive thoughts and big hugs your way.

Let me start saying: Allison, you rock!!!!!!!

Dear Super Woman,
The doctors are amazed at your progress, but all of us who have known you longer understand that, in the spirit of "you can't keep a good woman down," Allison O'Reilly won't stop until she has amazed the entire hospital staff.
It brought tears to my eyes today to hear that you were able to give Kevin the gift of an "I love you."

Sounds like you have landed in PT boot camp! You are such a determined person—they will not believe your will to succeed against all odds. Rock on, Al!

It is truly amazing and inspiring the number of lives you have touched! A true testament to you and how amazing you are! To this day you are still one of the (if not the) strongest, feistiest, most joyous, full-of-life and passionate women I have ever known—and I know without a doubt that you will overcome this. You are top of my thoughts and prayers as you fight through this.

You are the big sis God never gave me, and I owe so much to you and what I have come to learn from your tenacious, spunky heart. I know you will kick the crap out of this challenge and come out smelling like a rose.

I wanted you to know, that your husband, in your most urgent time of need, has inspired all of us with his love, devotion, and care for you. He has taken on the fight for you every step of the way, so that you only have to worry about using your gift of courage and tenacity to fight for your body to recover. Kevin never wavered, even if he did have to shed more than a few tears and share all of his fears with some of his closest friends. But, he has been strong, and now you will have to do the same.

Kevin has reached out to everyone he knows that loves you, and has asked them to pray for your fast recovery.

You have touched so many people with your warmth and radiance, and we hope you can feel our collective love and support now. You are an incredibly strong woman, and you will come out on the other side of this. Believe, and it will be.

You are one of the hardest working people I know—and you have the strength, ability, and spirit to overcome anything. Remember how many people love you and appreciate your friendship and your caring nature.

You have touched so many people, and each one of us is left better having met you. I hope now, at a time when you need us most, our admiration, friendship, and love for you gives you strength to persevere through this difficult time. You fight hard, girl—we all know you have it in you!!!!

I wasn't surprised by the outpouring of love you have received, I would expect nothing less for you!! The countless people who love and care for you will help support you. Please know that you are in everyone's thoughts.

These messages raised my spirits, kept me motivated (which I am anyway), and made me realize people care and love me, *despite* my stroke. I also think it made people realize how precious life is and that this just as easily could have happened to them.

Appendix

Things to Know about Stroke[15]

A stroke, sometimes called a brain attack, occurs when a clot blocks the blood supply to part of the brain or when a blood vessel in or around the brain bursts. In either case, parts of the brain become damaged or die. An *aneurysm* is caused by the ballooning of a localized area of a blood vessel. The bulge or ballooning of the vessels is usually found at the bottom or base of the brain. If you notice any signs or symptoms of a stroke, call 911 immediately (if you are somewhere other than North America, the emergency number might be different; when you travel, make sure you know what it is). *The chance that you will survive and recover from a stroke is higher if you get emergency treatment right away.* Stroke is the third leading cause of death worldwide, including in the United States.

For stroke survivors, recovery can take months or years. Many people who have had a stroke never fully recover.

Interesting Facts and Statistics about Stroke

The American Heart Association Statistics Committee and Stroke Statistics Subcommittee produce estimates and facts about stroke and other cardiovascular diseases in the United States. Below are some interesting facts about stroke, obtained from their 2007 report.

- What percent of adults from each race is affected by stroke?

  - American Indians/Alaska Natives: 5.3%

  - African Americans: 3.2%

  - Whites: 2.5%

  - Asians: 2.4%

- How many people suffer a stroke each year in the United States?

  - Each year 700,000 people suffer a stroke. Five hundred thousand of these strokes are first occurrences, while the rest are repeat strokes.

  - Every 45 seconds someone has a stroke in the United States.

- What are the most common types of stroke?

  - Ischemic strokes (restriction of blood flow to the brain) account for 87% of all strokes, while the other 13% are hemorrhagic strokes (bleeding inside the skull).

  - Up to 70% of strokes seen in the hospital are ischemic, while the remaining 30% are a mixture of transient ischemic attacks and hemorrhagic stroke.

    - Men

      1. thrombotic stroke: 61.5%

      2. embolic stroke: 23.5%

      3. intracerebral hemorrhage: 8.6%

      4. subarachnoid hemorrhage: 5.4%

      5. other: 1.1%

    - Women

      1. thrombotic stroke: 59%

      2. cerebral embolus: 26.2%

      3. intracerebral hemorrhage: 8.0%

      4. subarachnoid hemorrhage: 5.4%

      5. other: 1.3%

- What fraction of deaths in the United States is caused by stroke?

  - Stroke is the third most common cause of death in the United States.

  - Stroke accounts for about one of every sixteen deaths.

  - It causes a death every three to four minutes.

- How do people fare after a stroke?
  In one study performed six months after a stroke in people who were older than sixty-five years of age:

  - 30% needed assistance to walk;

  - 26% needed help with activities such as cooking, feeding, and paying their bills;

  - 19% had trouble speaking, or understanding others when they speak;

  - 35% had feelings of depression;

  - 50% had some degree of paralysis on one side of the body;

  - 26% became nursing home residents.

- What are the top 3 risk factors for stroke?

  - high blood pressure

  - diabetes

  - smoking

- How many people who suffer a stroke make it to the hospital on time to be treated?

  - Only 20% to 25% of patients who are admitted to the hospital with a stroke arrive in the emergency department within three hours of the onset of symptoms.

  - Fewer than 9% of ischemic strokes receive treatment with tissue plasminogen activator (TPA), a blood thinner.

- Other important statistics about stroke:

  - The risk for stroke in blacks is almost twice that of whites.

  - Over 43% of people over 85 have suffered a silent stroke.

  - The estimated total cost of stroke for 2007 is $62.7 billion.

  - Up to 40% of people in a recent study could not identify a single symptom. Each year, approximately 795,000 people suffer a stroke. About 600,000 of these are first attacks, and 185,000 are recurrent attacks.

  - Nearly three-quarters of all strokes occur in people over the age of 65. The risk of having a stroke more than doubles each decade after the age of 55.

- Strokes can and do occur at *any* age. Nearly one-fourth of strokes occur in people under the age of 65.

- Stroke death rates are higher for Americans of African descent than for whites, even at younger ages.

- On average, someone in the United States has a stroke every 40 seconds.

- Stroke accounted for about one of every 17 deaths in the United States in 2006. Stroke mortality for 2005 was 137,000.

- From 1995–2005, the stroke death rate fell 30%, and the actual number of stroke deaths declined 14%.

- The risk of ischemic stroke in current smokers is about double that of nonsmokers after adjustment for other risk factors.

- Atrial fibrillation (AF) is an independent risk factor for stroke, increasing risk about five-fold.

- High blood pressure is the most important risk factor for stroke.

Helping the Medical Industry Understand Strokes in Younger People

It is important for the medical industry to understand strokes are becoming more common in younger people, and they need to recommend rehab, not a nursing home. All a nursing home does is comfort you, and in younger people, there is still a life ahead. People have to be put in the right environment to thrive, and then recovery happens or it doesn't.

I know two other people who had strokes similar to mine and were also locked-in. They were 36 and 39. One is still locked-in. Another friend's brother, passed away at age 43.

My Medical Recap (June 2011)

Title: 49-Year-Old Female with Locked-In Syndrome with Significant Recovery

Authors: Lisa M. Maddox, MD (National Rehabilitation Hospital, Washington, DC), Victor Tseng, DO (National Rehabilitation Hospital), Brendan E. Conroy, MD (National Rehabilitation Hospital, Washington, DC)

Setting: Rehabilitation hospital

Patient: 49-year-old white female with tetraplegia, anarthria, and sustained consciousness.

Case Description: A very physically active 49-year-old, white female presented to her local emergency department with difficulty walking and swallowing. An MRI of the brain revealed a large brainstem infarct involving the bulk of the pons with extension to the anterior pontomedullary junction with extension to the low thalamus and broad involvement of the left low cerebellar hemisphere. Her neurologic examination deteriorated rapidly to her having no voluntary muscle movement except for vertical gaze. Due to an inability to swallow and manage her secretions, she underwent a tracheostomy and a percutaneous endoscopic gastrostomy. She was transferred from the acute hospital on the 11th day post-insult.

Discussion: LIS is an uncommon neurologic condition with a generally poor prognosis. The incidence and prevalence are difficult to quantify due to the imprecise use of the term when patients are diagnosed at acute hospitals. In this case, the patient had a true LIS. She underwent an intensive, multi-disciplinary treatment program.

Assessment/Results: The patient made significant progress during her 4-month admission to the acute rehabilitation hospital. At the time of discharge, the patient's functional status for activities of daily living ranged from contact-guard assistance to modified independence. The patient was able to ambulate more than 180 feet with a rolling walker and ankle-foot orthoses and negotiate a flight of stairs using 2 rails. She had mildly dysarthric speech and was discharged to home on a regular diet with thin liquids. The patient's cognition, awareness, and orientation remained intact throughout the entirety of her admission. She was actively included in the decision-making for her clinical care. After 2 months, the patient was able to communicate independently to her friends and family using a tablet computer and voice.

Conclusion: Locked-in syndrome should not routinely be considered a diagnosis requiring palliative care.

The ABCs for Survivors and Families

Advocate.

Be positive, be patient.

Caringbridge.org.

Don't give up.

Educate people on strokes.

Family and friends.

Give back.

Hold on to hope.

Indulge every once in a while—you deserve it.

Judge each person individually.

Keep the mind stimulated.

Love.

Make it happen.

Never give up.

Overcome/compensate for disabilities.

Push yourself.

Quality, not quantity in anything you do.

Rehab, rehab, rehab.

Strive to exceed your therapists' expectations.

Talk to the locked-in patient.

Understand stroke symptoms, so stroke can be ruled out.

Visualize yourself doing it.

Work hard.

Xcellence in all your efforts.

You are unique; every stroke is different.

Zero in on a goal.

Helpful Vocabulary[16]

ANGIOGRAPHY	Angiography is a test that uses an injection of a liquid dye to make the arteries easily visible on X-rays.
ATAXIA	Loss of the control of muscle function
ATHEROMA	Fatty deposits that build up inside an artery
ATRIAL FIBRILLATION	Heart condition in which the upper left side of the heart beats out of rhythm with the other three chambers. It increases the risk of a blood clot forming inside the heart, which can travel to the brain and cause a TIA or stroke.

AVM (Arterio-venous malformation)	Localized defects of the circulatory system, taking the form of tangled arteries and veins, that are generally believed to arise before or soon after birth. In most cases, there are no serious symptoms, but a small proportion lead to headaches, seizures, and even hemorrhage.
Berry Aneurysm	A bulge in the wall of an artery that is a weak
Broca's aphasia	Broca's aphasia, also known as non-fluent aphasia, is where a person has great difficulty speaking and can only manage to string a small number of words together in short, halting sentences. However, it is usually possible to understand the meaning of the sufferer's speech.
Bruit (Brewee)	The noise that can be heard when listening to a partially blocked blood vessel with a stethoscope
Carotid Endarterectomy	An operation performed to clear the inside of the carotid artery

CEREBELLUM	The cerebellum is the part of the brain involved in the coordination of voluntary motor movement, balance and equilibrium, and muscle tone
CEREBRAL ANGIOGRAM	A scan showing blood vessels in the brain
CEREBRUM	The main part of the brain, it is divided into left and right hemispheres.
CSF (CEREBROSPINAL FLUID)	A watery fluid surrounding the brain
CT SCAN	A type of X-ray. A CT scan stands for computed (or computerized) tomography scan. It is also known as a CAT (Computer Axial Tomography) scan. It is a medical imaging method that employs tomography. Tomography is the process of generating a two-dimensional image of a slice or section through a 3-dimensional object (a tomogram).
DVT (DEEP VEIN THROMBOSIS)	A clot of blood in the veins, usually of the leg
DYSARTHRIA	Speech disorder in which the pronunciation is unclear

DYSPHAGIA	Dysphagia is the medical term for the symptom of difficulty in swallowing.
DYSPHASIA	Aphasia is a communication disability which occurs when the communication centers of the brain are damaged. It is usually caused by stroke, but can also be caused by brain hemorrhage, head injury, or tumors. Aphasia is sometimes known as dysphasia. They both mean the same thing.
GAIT	The characteristics of walking particular to an individual
GLOBAL APHASIA	Global aphasia is the most severe form of aphasia/dysphasia. Someone with the condition has difficulty with all forms of communication, including speaking, reading, writing, correctly naming objects or people, and understanding other people's speech.
HEMIPLEGIA	Complete paralysis of half of the body

HUGHES SYNDROME	Also known as Primary Antiphospholipid Syndrome and *sticky blood syndrome*, people with it have an increased tendency to form clots in blood vessels.
HYDROCEPHALUS	Raised pressure within the skull due to an abnormal buildup of the fluid that surrounds the brain. It can occur after a brain hemorrhage and may be treated by the surgical placement of a shunt system.
INFARCTION	An area of cell death (e.g., part of the brain or part of the heart)
LACUNAR STROKE	A small stroke less than about one centimeter in diameter
NEUROPLASTICITY	Nerve cells that take over the function of other damaged cells
NYSTAGMUS	Involuntary jerking of the eyes that occurs in disorders of the part of the brain responsible for eye movements
OCCUPATIONAL THERAPIST (OT)	A therapist who specializes in helping people to reach their maximum level of function and independence in all aspects of daily life

Plaque	A mixture of fatty substances, including cholesterol and other lipids, deposited on the inside of artery walls
Shunt	A catheter (tube) that carries cerebrospinal fluid from a ventricle in the brain to another area of the body
Spatial Skills	Ability to judge depth, size, distance, and position in space
Stroke Unit	Hospital facility for the effective management of patients with acute stroke by a multi-disciplinary team of specialists
Thrombolysis	The use of drugs to break up a blood clot, a treatment which can be given to a minority of patients in the acute stage of ischemic stroke
Vertigo	An abnormal sensation of movement, spinning, tilting, or rocking, which may arise from damage to the brainstem or cerebellum. In other cases, it is due to middle-ear problems, and may be associated with tinnitus and hearing loss.

WARFARIN	The most frequently used oral anticoagulant (for thinning the blood and preventing clots forming inside the circulation)
WERNICKE'S APHASIA	Wernicke's aphasia, also known as fluent aphasia, is where a person is able to speak normally and use long, complex sentences, but the actual words used do not make sense, or nonsense words are included in the speech.

Helpful Websites

There are many useful sites; I have listed
just a few to help you get started.
www.medstarnrh.com
www.fightingstrokes.org
www.stroke.org
www.strokeassociation.org
www.caringbridge.org
www.stroke-survivors.co.uk

HUMAN BRAIN

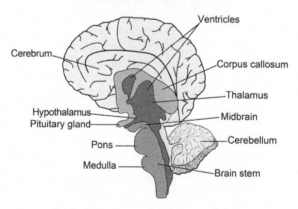

A diagram of the brain (courtesy of Shutterstock.com)

Notes

1. Jean-Dominique Bauby, *The Diving Bell and the Butterfly;* New York: A.A. Knopf: distributed by Random House, 1997.

2. Jawaharal Nehru, quoted in *Ignite the Fire Within* by Arthur J. Johnson II; Maitland, Florida: Xulon Press, 2004.

3. Proverb found in M. Broughton Boone's *Be the Butterfly;* Lulu.com, 2008.

4. Reese Flaxman quoting neuroscientist Dr. Andrew Clarkson in "New Strategies to Help Stroke Victims," Invercargill, NZ: *Southland Times;* 09/07/2013. http://www.stuff.co.nz/southland-times/your-newspaper/2634/Contact-The-Southland-Times. Accessed 09/07/2013.

5. Ali S. Saber Tehrani MD, Yu-Hsiang Hsieh PhD, MS, Georgios Mantokoudis MD, Frederick K. Korley MD, and Kevin D. Frick PhD, et al. "Johns Hopkins Study: Cost of Treating Dizziness in the Emergency Room Soars," Press Release 7/17/13. http://www.hopkinsmedicine.org/news/media/releases/johns_hopkins_study_cost_of_treating_dizziness_in_the_emergency_room_soars#.

6. For more information on LIS and Stroke, visit www.fightingstrokes.org. This website/charity was started by a thirty-nine-year old woman, Kate Allatt, from England, who was also locked-in and recovered.

7. Noted on www.stroke.org website.

8. Quoted from Nancy Futrell, MD, Vascular Neurology, Intermountain Stroke Center when she met me.

9. Knox, Richard, *NPR Health News*, April 2013. http://www.npr.org/blogs/health/2013/04/05/175682963/as-stroke-risk-rises-among-younger-adults-so-does-early-death.

10. *www.cdc.gov/vitalsigns/HeartDisease-Stroke/.*

11. *www.nrhrehab.org/Patient+Care/Inpatient/Stroke/default.aspx.*

12. *www.stroke.org/site/PageServer?pagename=pba.*

13. www.stroke.org/site/PageServer?pagename=faces_pba_home.

14. Kate Allatt, *Gonna Fly Now.* Printed and bound by CPI Group (UK) Ltd. Croydon, CR0 4YY, Self-published, 2012.

15. The American Heart Association Statistics Committee and Stroke Statistics Subcommittee.

16. Glossary from John D'Arcy at http://www.stroke-survivors.co.uk/stroke-glossary.aspx.

CPSIA information can be obtained
at www.ICGtesting.com
Printed in the USA
BVOW08s1220071117
499763BV00001B/89/P